Joe Public's Political Perspective

By

Billy Ray Chitwood

Copyright Page

Joe Public's Political Perspective is a work of non-fiction by Billy Ray Chitwood.

Cinc

831 Ridge View Drive

Spencer, Tennessee 38585

Cover design by JAC and CreateSpace

Copyright © 2013 by Cinc

ISBN-13:978-1494281908

ISBN-10:1494281902

ACKNOWLEGEMENT

The words in this book are mine, with a few exceptions here listed. I have used a 'Special Report' By Doug Bandow entitled 'America On Welfare' which appeared in The American Spectator last April, 2013. *The Great Society needs to be replaced by the Free Society.*

I have used an article by Wayne Allyn Root, which appeared in the *Las Vegas Review Journal* on April 3, 2013 and an e-mail sent to me referencing his words.

I have also used in my book's section on *Education* Wikipedia's information relative to school vouchers and educational tax credits.

These and any other source materials referenced or used were taken from the Internet. There has been no intention of skirting any law as it relates to using outside sources, considering that material on the internet is public access. If there has been an unintentional breach of etiquette and/or protocol relating to outside source information referenced in this book, I apologize.

DEDICATION

This book is dedicated to the brave and courageous military people who have answered their country's call, fought our wars, and have lost their lives so that a nation can live on and enjoy the freedom and liberty to pursue their many dreams and needs. May their collective efforts always stay alive in the hearts and minds of the men and women who wish to preserve the sacred document that our founding fathers so carefully and meticulously framed for us in the Constitution of the United States.

Books by Billy Ray Chitwood

Fiction

The Cracked Mirror – Reflections Of An Appalachian Son (A fictional memoir)

Mama's Madness

Butterflies and Jellybeans – A Love Story

The Reluctant Savage

The Bailey Crane Mystery Series

An Arizona Tragedy – A Bailey Crane Mystery (1)

Satan's Song – A Bailey Crane Mystery (2)

The Brutus Gate – A Bailey Crane Mystery (3)

Murder In Pueblo Del Mar – A Bailey Crane Mystery (4)

A Soul Defiled – A Bailey Crane Mystery (5)

Non-Fiction

What Happens Next? A Life's True Tale

Joe Public's Political Perspective

'Life is really simple… People insist on making it complicated.'

Anon

TABLE OF CONTENTS

Joe Public's Political Perspective

Preface

Which Joe Public? Do I mean the Joe Public whose views are moderate and/or in the center? Do I mean the Joe Public whose views are left or far left of center? Do I mean the Joe Public whose views are right or far right of center? Because the views held to the right of center seem to mirror those held by conservative folks, guess that's the Joe Public who is writing this relatively short composition.

Certainly I am not a journalist, a pundit, or a political analyst. There are many of those people around. There are many in-depth books that cover the views of one persuasion or another, replete with charts, graphs, facts and figures that make the mind reel. My simple perspective comes from many years of living in the United States, the land of my birth, and taking more than just a cursory and occasional look at what is happening inside the political arena.

It is understood that my thinking of what is right for our country will not fit another person's point of view. If I'm homeless, without a job and unwilling to really blister my feet in looking for a job and better living conditions, then I might certainly want the government to take care of my needs (food stamps and other welfare support).

Born into the lower class of the post-depression era I saw the ugliness of disease and poverty, was even a child of the state a couple of times until my good mother finally brought my sister and me back to a modest family home environment. With Mom's help, good luck, and the grace of God, I managed to get through that period, served in the US Navy, was honorably discharged, married, went to college, worked in the Credit Department of Sears and graduated with help from the GI Bill of Rights. So, I've been involved with some of government's welfare programs and have been thankful for them. Welfare might well be a necessary place to visit, but I certainly did not want to live there.

Speaking of experts, the pundits, and political analysts, you get a lot of information from them each and every day, depending on your television viewing channel choices. If you're like me these specialists can begin to sound scripted, like they are given by their particular powers of persuasion the catch phrases and summaries that we hear and see. It's okay to be organized and scripted, but there comes a time when the party lines get boring and one feels like we're not hearing the real story. That goes for both the major sides of political persuasion.

Admittedly and up front I admit to adopting some of the views I hold from what I hear, from books I have read, from what I have seen on television networks, and from what I have personally experienced in everyday living. This Joe Public has had no other sources from which to form the opinions I express here and has held no political office. Over the years I have settled on the side that makes sense to me, factoring in my psychological profile --- meaning my emotional makeup and my capacity for intelligent thinking. Like many citizens my participation in the country's affairs are reduced to social gatherings where there are generally like-minded friends and occasional opposing views. Over the years the conversations at these social affairs display some heated rhetoric and acrimony. But, the bottom line, my friends in the verbal battles and my foes never get worked up enough to strongly oppose, sign petitions for or against one political stance or another. We just let the elections come and go, make our voting preferences known in the voting booth, not vote at all, and get back into our routines.

I took great interest when Barack Obama ran for president the first time. He spoke of change and his words were most eloquent. Almost immediately I sensed that Mr. Obama was going to be the front runner on the Democratic ticket. His charismatic display and his stated vision for the country brought him followers and many dollars for his campaign. Even I listened closely to his words and almost believed what he was saying about change and a new direction. A southerner, I had never been bitten by the ugly bugs of racism and extreme bias. His color mattered not at all to me. In fact, I began to believe that this man might once and for all rip to shreds the race cards still held by many, might indeed be the man who would take the US to a new and better place.

Along came Joe the Plumber (Samuel Joseph Wurzelbacher) and made news with his remarks to then Senator Barack Obama during his campaign stops in his run for president. For those who do not remember, Joe the Plumber confronted Senator Obama with a question about the latter's small business tax policy. Senator Obama's response was, "When you spread the wealth around, it's good for everybody." This became good fodder for the Republican campaign of John McCain as an indicator that Obama had socialist leanings and was interested in the redistribution of wealth. Joe went on to become an American conservative activist, commentator, and motivational speaker. Joe also ran in Ohio's 9th Congressional District's 2012 race for the House of Representatives and lost to an incumbent democrat. Joe did not have the big D machine behind him. I mention this good middle-class American because he got involved and tried to make a difference.

Joe the Plumber's remarks and subsequent arguments by the GOP group gave me pause and I was on the proverbial fence. While I did not vote for Mr. Obama, I suggested to my conservative friends that we needed to give Mr. Obama a chance, that maybe he would be good for the country. Those initial suggestions had life for just a few short months. My bubble burst rather quickly.

Whether or not my ramblings here have any interest or make any sense to the reader, my words still give me some satisfaction. Obviously, my words do not have the same resonance as the pundits and political specialists.

My words of course do matter to me and I feel they will resonate with millions of others across our great land. When the real urge hit me to write my thoughts I decided to leave civility behind and say exactly what was on my mind.

The people who made that decision easy for me were particularly Harry Reid, Nancy Pelosi, and the president himself. It is at least evident to me these people talk civility but do not particularly participate in the act itself. There are other names from both sides of the political aisle that could be mentioned but these are the first to come to me…and, to my mind, the most egregious.

My reflections, like most, are taken from various sources, what I read, what I see, to whom I talk. Having absorbed through the years so many different political views on various subjects, I have come to the conclusions reflected here. Hopefully my words will not be read as arrogant, pompous, and/or pedantic. Most likely, this book is the result of too much absorption in an area that creates anger, angst, and anxiety. However, I care about my country, my children, grandchildren, and those to follow, and I wish them to know how I feel about this particular era in our history. Freedom and Liberty have been forged here. We cannot let them get away from us.

Who do we believe when we have relevant issues being dissected by so many? What actions are espoused more reasonably, more truthfully? What are we the people expected to do other than trust those we elect to handle our myriad problems? How do we build a fire under those of us who take no interest in the future welfare of our country? There are so many arcane variables at play in our society that make the understanding of political matters difficult at best and boring at worse. There is no way to force a person to become engaged and get interested in political matters. But, most certainly, we have an electorate that will lead us one way or another.

What amazes me the most is that, among those of us who are engaged in the issues facing the country and the world, we can be so far apart in our thinking. There are those with special agendas for remaking our country into something our founding fathers surely never intended. There are those who lie to us or show us false data. It has become so easy to corrupt honesty, or, has it always been so? Is my naïveté showing?

Through all my meandering thoughts here, all I want are honest people running our country, telling us the truth and being transparent with us (unless, of course, national security issues prevent such clarity), crossing party lines to do what reason dictates is honorable and right.

So, I'm just a guy who spent his youth and many of his middle years not being too concerned about the affairs of my country and my world. A light went on somewhere along my way and I began to see the 'special interest' aspects in our government, the fraud, the wasteful spending of tax-payer dollars, the 'scripts' each political party uses to counter this or promote that, the threats to our freedom and liberty by certain actions and/or legislation. In short, somewhere along the way I became more concerned. What kind of country did I want to live in? Was it true that our government was actually considering turning our free enterprise system into more tightly controlled bureaucracies that would stifle creativity, hard work, incentive, and touch so many aspects of our lives? Were the quick knowledge explosions brought by computers, electronic devices, social networking, all the technological and scientific advances creating not a brave new world but one of dependency and shallow human effort? I became concerned about so many things…

All my concerns brought periods of anger and dismay. Inevitably, at social functions, conversations would come up about politics. Not only did I see my own anger rising but I saw it in the faces and tones of others. So I leave civility at the door (as it seems many of our politicians have) and simply write what is in my heart and mind, understanding that with these words I create enemies and some new friends.

I've lived a long life, still too sensitive for my own good, but my days of catering to beliefs counter to my own are past. While I speak from a point of honest feeling and thought, I realize most abundantly that I'm no expert on any subject, that there is persuasion on both sides of the political spectrum. Nonetheless, I have chosen my side of the aisle. Yet, without public recognition or any agenda, I write this merely as a citizen of the United States, the greatest nation on earth.

My political perspective is directed in the areas which I call: 1) The Real State of Our Union; 2) Security at Home and Abroad; 3) The Economy; 4) Guns and Gun Control; 5) The Criminal Justice System; 6) Education; 7) Capitalism and the Free Enterprise System; 8) The War on Terror and Islam – Past Reflections; 9) Religion and Faith; 10) The Secular Mindset; 11) Where Do You Want To Go From Here?; 12) Some Last Thoughts.

JOE PUBLIC'S POLITICAL PERSPECTIVE

1) The Real State of Our Union

Each year we are treated to some pomp and ceremony called *The State of the Union* address. Call me nuts but I enjoy these moments where history plays out its old time honored tradition, where there comes the anticipation of those words: "The President of the United States." While the President makes his way through the throng of dignitaries, shaking hands, kissing cheeks, whispering words in the ears of some, smiling and waving his arms. It takes some time for the Commander In Chief to reach the podium, to shake the hands of the vice-president and the Speaker of the House, to present the golden envelopes to each. The applause goes on and on until the Speaker of the House announces once again, "Members of Congress, I have the high privilege and distinct honor of presenting to you the President of the United States." The applause again goes on and on, with the President's faithful mass standing and showing their pearly whites… All, such wonderful drama!

Then the words that are to bring clarity about our nation's affairs begin…"My Fellow Americans…"

The words flow, often beautifully articulated and usually more positive in tenor and rhetoric than many in the great hall and at home would agree. They are words, just as these written symbols are my words, seeking agreement and consensus that never truly comes in the numbers wished by the speaker and/or writer. But words are what we humans use to express our beliefs, our ideas, our dreams and hopes. It is left to the listener and the reader of words to determine the sincerity, the truth and the factual viability of words.

As President Obama orates grandly to his audience of government officials, to the influential among the assemblage, and to his vast television audience, he sounds impassioned and sincere. He speaks of the work that congress needs to get done. He gives us data and figures taken from a particular poll or government source to back-up the claims he is making. His 'left' side of the aisle stands and applauds when he makes a partisan point favorable to his cause, while the 'right' side might emit some low grumbling sounds. The President claims gains in the economy, more jobs being created, our troops coming home from Afghanistan, American prestige still at a high point among the nations of the world. He deflects deftly or mentions not at all some of the most important issues on which his critics have assailed him.

At the end of the President's 'State of the Union' address, there is the applause and the handshakes as he goes from the hallowed hall as he came, smiling, patting backs, thanking supporters here and there, and giving secretive little winks and nods to certain people in the crowd.

There is then a transition to the Cable and primetime Networks that form their panels to digest for the viewers the substance of the President's speech. There will also be a minority party speaker to voice his/her remarks about the 'State of the Union' address to the country, intent on making their comments mostly non-conciliatory.

So, what exactly is the 'State of the Union' to Joe Public?

Not since slavery was abolished and the great Civil War, it is my belief that few can argue with the fact that our country, The United States of America, is in its most ominous and precarious position – certainly, in my lifetime. There are many reasons for this, not the least of which is the digital world in which we live, where practically anything goes. Individuals and politically controlled groups can Tweet or Facebook their messages to the world, and there is no moral obligation to be respectful and truthful.

One can harass and psychologically impair a young person on the internet to the point of suicide. Pedophiles can practice satanic deeds, disguising their true intents by using false and misleading information. Pornography is rampant on the websites of America. Gangsters, murderers, white-collar criminals, can hatch their evil plans with easy pecking of their laptops.

It is more than a suggestion, but I believe the internet provided a huge boost to Barack Obama's relatively easy victory over Mitt Romney in 2012. The democrats made excellent use of their expertise in this medium. I'm not discounting the entitlement constituency and the minority groups, but the internet was most effectively used by the democratic machine. By far, however, the votes that gave victory to Obama were from those who believe that Mom and Pop Government can satisfy their needs from cradle to grave.

Of course, it is more than the speedy electronic age in which we're living. Really, when one looks at the diversity of cultures and nations around the world, how do we all come together? Is it viable to even think along those lines? Unless some magical elixir is invented that takes language and culture to some ridiculous parity and every human being is forced to consume it, we are tantamount to forcing a square peg into a round hole. That is, perhaps it would be better to keep a close 'security eye' on the rest of the world and concentrate on making our own nation economically healthy and too strong of might that any other country would dare to reckon with us.

Perhaps it would be better to stay the course of our Constitution, keep Capitalism and the Free Enterprise System firmly in place without toying with things like 'Redistribution of Wealth', government funding businesses, and a huge government welfare system. If we have incentive to work, to invest and create new businesses and jobs, people who want to work will find work.

Do our people really understand 'Redistribution of Wealth' and the not so subtle effects it could and will have on the country? The 'Affordable Healthcare Act' is a perfect example of the 'Redistribution' concept.

(NOTE: in other parts of this book, I may refer to the Affordable Healthcare Act as AHA or ACA (Affordable Care Act.)

The Affordable Healthcare Act is a massive piece of legislation put together by the Democratic Party and it has all the smoke and mirrors which will likely lead our country so far off course we might not be able to find our way back. How do I know this? There is no absolute in my knowing this, but I do have respect and trust in the people most close to it that speak of its costs and mandates. Plus, I know of no government Bureaucracy that can or has run smoothly over the years.

Have I laboriously read the act's pages? No, I've only read snatches of it here and there. With what I've seen of the Act and the reports from those people I respect and trust, this is a boondoggle of the first order. There will be fewer doctors to care for our people. There will be additional costs added periodically as the legislation moves along. There is simply the idea that a huge bureaucracy has been created, and by now we should all know **how not very well** these 'monsters' work.

The 'redistribution of wealth' aspect of the Act comes via the mandates within the government offered plans in the AHA 'health insurance market place' on the internet. Regardless of plan selected the enrollee will be paying much more in costs than they previously paid. Each plan has its coverage mandates, like maternity benefits, contraceptives, et al. Let's say you are fifty-five, have no need of the 'maternity mandated coverage', you will still get it and pay for it if you choose that plan.

The idea is that the younger people among us will have to buy government plans or be fined. Many will pay the fine and reject the coverage, causing the costs to eventually go even higher. So, the majority of the people will be paying higher costs for their insurance plans so that the government can provide free coverage for the relatively small percentage of minorities and people who cannot afford insurance coverage, many of whom now benefit from government programs already in place. This government then takes its 'big ticket' money and redistributes it in the form of subsidies to the poorer people among us. The thought may be noble but it undermines programs already in place for the poor and leads us toward an uncertain future.

The most unappealing and arrogant aspect of this bureaucratic nightmare is that this administration is telling its people (we the people) that it knows best what we need to be doing.

I have likely missed an element or two, but you get the idea. The tax payers of our country will bear the extra costs of ObamaCare for the relatively few people it could possibly benefit.

As you will see this repeated a number of times in this book, we must help those who cannot honestly and truly help themselves, but I submit to you that it is wrong to bankrupt a nation and its majority in the process. On its surface, from all that I read and see, that is where this Affordable Healthcare Act is leading us.

Why is it so difficult to understand that we cannot make everyone equal, financially and otherwise? There are too many variables to overcome – intelligence, work ethic, bad genes, criminality, on and on…unless, of course, someone is hiding that magical potion in some vault that can make the good fairy touch us all with her baton.

Take a close look at this 'Special Report' by Doug Bandow. It was written last April, 25, 2013 in the 'American Spectator.' It is a conservative paper, but it is factual.

*

SPECIAL REPORT

America on Welfare

By DOUG BANDOW on 4.25.13 @ 6:09AM

The Great Society needs to be replaced by the Free Society.

Living the good life on welfare. Even the Europeans recognize that they pay a high price for creating an increasingly dependent society.

Denmark has been transfixed by the revelation of a 36-year-old single mother who collects more in benefits than many Danes earn at work, and has done so for two decades. *Worried Karen Haekkerup, Minister of Social Affairs and Integration, people "think of these benefits as their rights. The rights have just expanded and expanded."*

But it's really not that much different in the U.S., the nominal home of the free. Nearly two decades ago welfare reform briefly captured political attention and won bipartisan support. The effort was a great success. But most welfare programs remained untouched and the gains have been steadily eroded.

Today nearly 48 million people, almost one out of every six Americans, receive Food Stamps. Outlays on this program alone have quadrupled in just a decade. Indeed, the government actively promotes the program, encouraging people to sign up. Other welfare programs also are growing in reach and cost. The Congressional Budget Office recently pointed to "increases in the number of people participating in those programs and increases in spending per participant." The U.S. isn't that far behind Europe.

Indeed, America, like Europe, has a veritable welfare industry. A forthcoming <u>report</u> from the <u>Carleson Center for Public Policy</u>, named after Reagan administration welfare chief Robert Carleson, charges that "The federal government has spawned a vast array of redundant, overlapping and poorly targeted assistance programs." Authors Susan Carleson and John Mashburn count 157 means-tested programs intended to alleviate poverty. There were more than two score housing programs, more than a score of nutrition programs, almost as many employment/training and health programs, and lesser numbers of cash assistance, community development, and disability programs. More expansive definitions count even more programs — 185 total, according to Peter Ferrara.

No surprise, the welfare industry is expensive. Social Security is the single most costly program, but more goes collectively to welfare. Today government at all levels spends around $1 trillion a year on means tested anti-poverty programs. And that amount is just going up and up.

Total federal and state welfare spending rose from $431 billion in 2000 to $927 billion in 2011. Both parties are responsible, but President Obama bears particular responsibility. Last year, explained my Cato Institute colleague Michael Tanner: "Welfare spending increased significantly under President George W. Bush and has exploded under President Barack Obama. In fact, since President Obama took office, federal welfare spending has increased by 41 percent, more than $193 billion per year."

And this is just the start. From 2009 to 2018, figured Heritage Foundation scholars Robert Rector, Katherine Bradley, and Rachel Sheffield, at current rates the federal government will spend $7.5 trillion and states *will spend $2.8 trillion on welfare, for a total of $10.3 trillion.*

Washington can ill afford such expenditures. Uncle Sam ran more than $5 trillion in deficits over the past four years and is expected to run up a deficit of $845 billion this year. The Congressional Budget Office recently warned that while deficits are expected to decline over the next two years, they then will start rising again to $1 trillion annually. Over the next decade, assuming unrealistically that Congress doesn't add any new programs or increase outlays for any old ones, the accumulated red ink will be $7.0 trillion.

Alas, this is merely the brief break before the tsunami of entitlement outlays hits. The total unfunded liability for Social Security and Medicare exceeds $100 trillion. To that must be added a long list of contingent, likely, and potential liabilities. Even the Post Office is broke and needs a bail-out! Economist Laurence Kotlikoff estimated total federal indebtedness at an astonishing $222 trillion.

Despite facing financial doom, government provides welfare to "a growing number of people who increasingly are not 'needy' by any rational definition," write Carleson and Mashburn. Wasteful duplication isn't limited to welfare, of course. Yet abuse of programs supposedly directed at human needs seems especially odious. There are people in need. In their name government is taxing away people's earnings and wasting the proceeds.

It's important not to focus solely on money. If the programs worked the amount being spent might not seem so excessive. However, observed Tanner, last year the nearly $1 trillion spent on welfare amounted "to $20,610 for every poor person in America, or $61,830 per poor family of three." With that kind of spending, no one should still be poor.

Yet when testifying before Congress in 2011, Patricia Dalton of the General Accountability Office refused to "hazard a guess" as to what percentage of federal welfare programs achieved their objectives. She admitted that it "would be good to have a number of how many programs there are, what exactly are we spending, and what are we getting for that money." Yes, that would be good.

Unfortunately, over the years it became increasingly evident that welfare did much to discourage marriage and work, and destroy family and community. That is, behavioral poverty accompanied material poverty. The result, complained the Heritage Foundation's Robert Rector and Jennifer Marshall, "has been the disintegration of the work ethic, family structure, and social fabric of large segments of the American population, which has in turn created a new dependency class." This directly threatens the American vision of self-government by independent citizens.

Yet the system is tenaciously defended by all of the usual interest groups which benefit from extensive federal wealth transfers. President Reagan argued that "The war on poverty created a great new upper-middle class of bureaucrats that found they had a fine career as long as they could keep enough needy people there to justify their existence." Officials may not exactly scheme to prevent the poor from leaving welfare. But welfare gives many people an interest in preserving existing programs.

One of Reagan's most notable achievements as two-term governor of California was confronting the seemingly unconstrained growth of welfare spending. Aided by Carleson, Gov. Reagan also opposed proposals by Presidents Lyndon Johnson and Richard Nixon for a guaranteed national income.

Reagan took center political stage when he was elected president in 1980. He brought Carleson to Washington and chose as his domestic policy adviser Hoover Institution scholar Martin Anderson, another trenchant critic of the Johnson-Nixon approach. Reagan made welfare reform one of his priorities, explaining: "States are better equipped than the federal government to administer effective welfare reforms if they are given broad authority to utilize administrative and policy discretion." However, the House remained in Democratic hands and welfare remained largely unchanged.

Still, the debate gradually shifted. Charles Murray's Losing Ground: American Social Policy 1950-1980 crystallized the national realization that welfare wasted lives as well as money. When Republicans took control of both houses of Congress in 1994, welfare reform became a priority.

In 1996 President Bill Clinton signed legislation that turned Aid to Families with Dependent Children into Temporary Assistance to Needy Families. Federal matching grants became fixed block grants, with time limits and work requirements. The reform, explain Carleson and Mashburn, "reversed 61 years of U.S. welfare policy by ending a recipient's automatic entitlement to a cash welfare check. It was a good start, one on which Congress and the state legislatures can build a better future for millions of people still trapped by the incentives for dependency that remain in the remnants of the old welfare system."

It was a very good start. Millions of people were moved off welfare rolls into the workplace. Even many opponents of the legislation were forced to acknowledge the positive results. The good economy was important. But more important was the fact that recipients could no longer in effect marry welfare. TANF was determined to minimize both behavioral and material poverty.

However, the remnants that Carleson and Mashburn speak of remain a significant problem. As Elliott Gaiser recently observed in calling for further welfare reform, "the '96 welfare reform really only fixed one" program, AFDC. There are 156 to go! Moreover, the Democratic Congress and President Barack Obama together weakened the 1996 reforms, risking a slide back to a 1960s welfare dependency mentality. For instance, complain Carleson and Mashburn: "the Obama administration's policies have lured tens of millions of people onto the Food Stamp rolls, while loosening eligibility requirements for welfare programs across the board."

The way back won't be easy. America has spent decades creating the dependency-inducing welfare industry. The ultimate objective should be to reinforce and rebuild, when necessary the traditional emphasis on personal, family, and community responsibility.

Indeed, this model of outward moving concentric rings of responsibility goes back to the Bible. Individuals were expected to work if possible, and not burden others. The Apostle Paul explained that a Christian who "failed to provide for his relatives, and especially his immediate family" was "worse than an unbeliever" (1Timothy 5:8). The ancient Israelites and New Testament Christians alike created rules and procedures to aid those in need within their communities of faith. Finally, Paul wrote, "as we have opportunity, let us do good to all people" (Gal. 6:10).

Any government role should start only when private provision proves inadequate, and even then begin at the local and state levels. The national government should be the last, not first, resort. Even now we see some government efforts at reform, but primarily outside of Washington. For instance, Wisconsin Gov. Scott Walker plans to require work or job training to receive Food Stamps (now officially called the Supplemental Nutrition Assistance Program).

Carleson and Mashburn detail a state-based strategy in their new study, "Secure the Safety Net: Repeal and Replace the Welfare State." They look back past the 1996 reforms to Ronald Reagan's experience in California.

Welfare wasn't always viewed as Washington's job. Observe Carleson and Mashburn: "Welfare once was the province of the states, but increasingly has been treated as a federal responsibility. Since the 1960s, when the concept of public welfare radically expanded, federal micromanagement and redistribution of income has grown out of control." The most important first step that we could take is to push the welfare mass/mess back to the states.

Carleson and Mashburn propose eliminating 30 programs costing $849 million and consolidating into block grants another 127 programs costing $530 billion. More specifically, they would create seven block grants: community development, absorbing *eight programs; cash assistance, replacing 11 programs; disability, transforming Supplemental Security Income for the Disabled; employment and training, consolidating 19 programs; housing, replacing 46 programs; medical assistance, incorporating 18 existing programs; and nutrition, consolidating 24 programs.*

Equally important, the grants would be fixed, with a congressional vote required for any funding increase, and largely unrestricted, with federal oversight limited to audits of expenditures. Explain Carleson and Mashburn, transferring funds directly from the U.S. Treasury "would end federal, 'Washington-knows-best' bureaucratic interference and overreach. Governors would be able to design unified welfare systems tailored to best meet the needs of their low-income citizens."

Obviously states are not perfect and their reputation suffered badly during the Civil Rights era. However, today states are by far more responsible, responsive, and innovative than the national government. The Great

Society needs to be replaced by the Free Society. Shifting power and responsibility out of Washington would begin what inevitably will be a lengthy and difficult process.

The current welfare system obviously is bad for taxpayers. It also is bad for poor people. Reform is desperately needed. Congress could begin the process tomorrow by turning national programs into state block grants. America can't afford to wait.

(Mr. Bandow is a member of the Carleson Center's Policy Board.)

*

Here is my admission, I (Joe Public) am not much of a fact and figures guy and I realize that my emotions get in the way. Mr. Bandow's article in the 'American spectator' should provide enough factual data to get across what I believe to be the 'State of Our Union' at the present time. When you have more people on welfare than are working it is crisis time. It is particularly crisis time if you believe in freedom, liberty, and the pursuit of happiness.

When considering our new Affordable Care Act (ObamaCare), I can get very emotional. No, I have not read this entire mass of 'fine print' requirements and gobbledygook, but enough facts and cost data have surfaced that it makes me shudder with outrage. It is my belief that very few people have read it, including those in the congress and the President himself. In my opinion, this 'smoke and mirrors' legislation is the most mammoth and the most disturbing piece of law this nation has ever seen. (Yes, I'm sure some of FDR's 'New Deal' reforms might have appeared mammoth and disturbing at its time – but not to this extent.)

ObamaCare is a law that so many people do not understand. It was written in a Democrat-controlled house and senate at the dictates of Barack Obama and cohorts Nancy Pelosi and Harry Reid. The vote for the bill was across straight party lines. All republicans voted nay. All democrats voted yea. I have yet to find any citizen who understands this law, and I shall never forgive Chief Justice John Roberts for putting his deciding stamp of approval on the law. Like so many others I believe this cumbersome piece of legislation takes us further down the road toward Socialism.

If the law itself were not enough to create the nation's deep doubt, consider the rollout debacle of the Act with its faulty unworkable website and the chaos and costs it has brought. Consider the Secretary of Health and Human Resources, Kathleen Sebelius, with 3 ½ years to prepare for this rollout and she could not get it done. Consider the near billion dollar cost to the US tax payers of this launch of ACA (just the rollout itself). It appears that the firm hired by HHS to build this website and failed has now been re-hired to try again --- and, or course, for more money. Consider the privacy issues raised by the website, where there apparently are none. No tests were done. No privacy protection for users. Consider the vetting process of the navigators hired for the website…no in-depth probes into their backgrounds and clearance protocol lax or non-existent.

To be fair, there are some good parts to ObamaCare. The 'Pre-existing conditions section' has obvious merit. Not losing your insurance if and when you change jobs is an important feature. Being able to keep your children on the insurance is appealing. Certainly, the ACA helps the poor among us, and that is good… But, could we not have addressed all these areas in private legislation instead of creating a government bureaucracy? The government has proven time and again that their bureaucratic machinery does not work well at all --- considering all the billions in fraud and wasteful spending that is done each year. Again, to be fair, there are some things that the government does well, but creating businesses and bureaucracies are not among them. In short, the government should leave business to the private sector and concentrate in those areas laid out in our Constitution.

Those of us who never wanted ObamaCare, who would like it repealed and new private sector changes made to healthcare, do not, should not, see this ill-fated launch to ObamaCare as a victory for the Republican Party. We must remember that we have a president who is charismatic and can keep repeating deceptive words to those who think him infallible: "If you have an insurance plan you like, you can keep it…period!" "A doctor you like, you can keep her/him!" he has made these statements repeatedly in defense of his legacy legislation. Now, as people are losing their insurance coverage because of the mandates in his Act, he still dances around the truth of his socialistic boondoggle. These words were uttered years before and during the 2012 presidential campaign and just possibly won Obama his second term…that, the timing of Hurricane Sandy, and Romney's relaxed position on Benghazi in the third presidential debate. (It now appears there could have been some fudging on the 'employment numbers' in Obama's favor as the presidential race tightened in October of 2012 – where the numbers of the unemployed were reported at 7.8 % when they were really over the 8 % mark… To be fair, at this writing, this information has not been validated. We do know for a fact that Obama used the 7.8 % unemployment number in his campaign speeches.)

The scariest thing about the Affordable Care Act is the direction it is taking this country.

Health care accounts for one-sixth of our economy, and we can already see how the government runs a business. That's because Obama and many in government have never run a business. Obama might have run his Senate office the short time he was there, but he has no experience and neither do some other career politicians.

There's so much to be concerned about if you are truly concerned about this great country of ours. Just recently, Obama's White House has put limits on the media's rights to ask certain questions at press conferences – those certain questions purportedly have to do with classified matters, but other matters have not been ruled out. It appears the White House will do its own producing of facts to be delivered to the public.

Does it all sound just a wee bit scary for our democracy? It indeed does for this Joe Public.

A Scottish Professor once wrote about the life of a democracy:

*

In 1887 Alexander Tyler, a Scottish history professor at the University of Edinburgh, had this to say about the fall of the Athenian Republic some 2,000 years prior: "A democracy is always temporary in nature; it simply cannot exist as a permanent form of government. A democracy will continue to exist up until the time that voters discover that they can vote themselves generous gifts from the public treasury. From that moment on, the majority always votes for the candidates who promise the most benefits from the public treasury, with the result that every democracy will finally collapse over loose fiscal policy, (which is) always followed by a dictatorship."

"The average age of the world's greatest civilizations from the beginning of history has been about 200 years. During those 200 years, these nations always progressed through the following sequence:

From bondage to spiritual faith;
From spiritual faith to great courage;
From courage to liberty;
From liberty to abundance;

From abundance to complacency;
From complacency to apathy;
From apathy to dependence;
From dependence back into bondage."

The Obituary follows: Born 1776, Died 2016

It doesn't hurt to read this several times.

*

Add this to the above information:

Professor Joseph Olson of Hamline University
School of Law in St. Paul, Minnesota, points
out some interesting facts concerning the last
Presidential election:

*-Number States won by: Obama: 19; Romney
29*
*-Square miles of land won by: Obama: 580,000;
Romney: 2,427,000*
*-Population of counties won by: Obama: 127
million; Romney: 143 million*
*-Murder rate per 100,000 residents in counties
won by: Obama: 13.2; Romney: 2.1*

Professor Olson adds: "In aggregate, the map of the territory Romney won was mostly the land owned by the taxpaying citizens of the country.

Obama territory mostly encompassed those citizens living in low income tenements and living off various forms of government welfare..."

*Olson believes the United States is now somewhere between the "complacency and apathy" phase of Professor Tyler's definition of democracy, with some **forty percent** of the nation's population*
already having reached the "governmental dependency" phase.

If Congress grants amnesty and citizenship to twenty million criminal invaders called illegals - and they vote - then we can say goodbye to the USA in fewer than five years.

*

Our forefathers wrote a document called The **Constitution**, a document that was methodically and meticulously thought out, a document which should if followed make it exempt to the Scottish Professor's thesis. So, if we can fight off the secular onrush and dictum of 'anything goes' and maintain our religious and fundamental rights, we can endure until the final roll is called.

Can it not be relatively simple? Cut the size of our government? Give States more control? Make sure we take care of those who truly need our help – not the people who thrive through fraudulent claims and make dependency a way of life? Can we not get some good honest people to run our central government? People who will keep us safe and secure? People who will not succumb to the greed of money and power? Too simple-minded, you say. Perhaps that is so but our people must somehow regain that 'great generation' mentality and spirit, force those in our halls of congress to not favor themselves with gifts and benefits that we the people do not have.

There is hope and great anticipation that our country will do what is necessary to change the current State of Our Union. It will take courage and fortitude on the part of our chosen leaders and representatives to start the roll-back of a cumbersome federal government bureaucracy that benefits the elite who built their self-serving power bases but demoralizes and destroys motivation and success for so many.

JOE PUBLIC'S POLITICAL PERSPECTIVE

2) Security At Home and Abroad

While so many voices scream for 'Gun Control' poison gas takes lives in Syria and thousands of AK-47s are used in the streets Syria, Afghanistan, Iraq, Iran, Libya, Egypt, Benghazi, Somalia, throughout the Middle East and Africa, not to mention Latin America and the United States. It would be so mercifully perfect were we able to collect all guns of every type, all weapons of mass destruction, and destroy them, as with nuclear bombs, poison gas…and hatred. Guess what? It is not possible! Guns and weaponry of all kinds are all around us, and it is not those guns and weaponry that kill human beings. Human beings kill human beings. It is the warped mind filled with anger and hatred that uses these weapons for the annihilation of people…a sad but unalterable truth.

Why is it such a difficult truth to accept? Our Second Amendment to the US Constitution gives our citizens the right to bear arms, to protect their families, to hunt and provide sustenance, to enjoy recreational shooting. Reasonable laws should of course be in place to insure compliance in the use and handling of a firearm, in registering firearms, and signed acknowledgements to these facts. No person with a felony criminal record should be allowed the use of firearms, having forfeited their rights to use by their prior felonious actions.

Our homeland security measures carry some distaste to many of our people, but extraordinary means must be taken in fighting terrorists without uniforms whose deep hatred for America is firm and inalterable. Encroachment on some of our liberties might be necessary at times to keep us safe. For me, that is a small adjustment to make for keeping my head and my family's head firmly attached to the body. We don't have to be so pure in our devotion to our sacred documents that we would cease to exist by staying true to them. All those who have died on battlefields around the world to protect us and keep us safe would not want it otherwise. My Faith is intact but it does not take me to that place of propitiation.

We fight an enemy like no other we have ever known. This enemy is a radical hate machine without any code of military justice. This enemy perceives us as infidels deserving of death. This enemy will die for some glorious reward that awaits them in an afterlife filled with virgins. This enemy has hated, fought, killed since the Biblical tribes dispersed and promulgated their beliefs. This enemy wishes to control the world. This enemy uses the word Jihad to describe its holy war against unbelievers of Islam and sees it as their duty to purify the world of infidels. All of Islam does not fight and hate, but enough of them do that make it necessary for us to reexamine the way we need to respond to terrorist actions.

My Faith does not allow me to turn the other cheek in this War on Terror. All I need to ask myself about interrogation techniques that could elicit information about an impending attack is this thought: *My children, my grandchildren could be in harm's way. If water-boarding, ear-splitting sound torture, other non-life threatening techniques, can be used to*

determine the time and place of a terrorist
action, Use Them!

This is common sense, not Political Science
101. Who among the sane and sensible can
believe in a Deity that wants people's heads
severed? I want my government to use every
experienced security mind in our country to
come up with a fail safe system for protecting
out citizens at home. Not many of us are sitting
in on National Security Council Meetings and
Top Secret briefings, so I realize the naïve
nature of some of my comments. However, I am
able to read, to see and absorb the news events
of the day, and I believe that President Obama
has done some good things in the War On
Terror – taking out Osama Bin Laden, the drone
attacks, and, very likely, some secret missions
we are not allowed nor supposed to know about.

Conversely, President Obama has, in my
opinion, made some bad calls. First and
foremost, I believe the President has appointed
inept people to some very important posts in our
government. What is the magic of Hilary
Clinton? I see none at all, but that's perhaps too

biased and too uninformed an opinion. As Secretary of State, what were her accomplishments? I see none, but then maybe I'm just being unfair. She was absent when four good people were killed in a Benghazi embassy attack on 9/11/2012 (the date sound familiar?), claiming it was a simple protest to some video that was unkind to Islam. At the same time, the President was taking a campaign trip to Nevada. After a year, the American people have still not been briefed on Benghazi and the reasons so little was done and reported about the event. To the President's credit, he did replace Hilary Clinton with John Kerry as Secretary of State – at this point in time, Mr. Kerry has acquitted himself well.

I can also speak of other cabinet members and appointees of President Obama who appear to have checkered pasts and very little to offer in the way of experience, at least, from what I have heard and read. It is really tough to listen to a press conference as Jay Carney mumbles and stumbles through some significant queries by the White House corps of reporters.

President Obama has charisma and is an excellent orator. He is likable and intelligent. It is my feeling that he believes in his vision for America. There is nothing wrong with helping those in our country who need assistance, through no fault of their own. The President errs when he believes that taking money from those who work and pay taxes should be redistributed to even the playing field. In my opinion, the President is playing a role he has no right to play. The playing field will never be level. We will always have those movers and shakers who want to build a business, to invest in companies where they see potential, and we well always have the unfortunate few who cannot make it on their own because of education, genetics, health problems, age, or lack of ambition. The government should provide the people with good security at home and abroad, allow for safe-guard regulations for businesses, but leave business to fail or foster in the private sector.

I include here an article, 'A Gorilla in the Room', written by Wayne Allyn Root in the Las Vegas Review Journal on April 3, 2013. Mr. Root was a '83 classmate of Barack Obama at

Columbia University. It is important food for thought:

*

by Wayne Allyn Root

(Las Vegas Review-Journal, April, 3 2013)

Barack Hussein Obama is no fool. He is not incompetent. On the contrary, he is brilliant. He knows exactly what he's doing. He is purposely overwhelming the U.S. economy to create systemic failure, economic crisis and social chaos thereby destroying capitalism and our country from within. Barack Hussein Obama was my college classmate (Columbia University , class of '83).

*He is a devout Muslim; do not be fooled. Look at his czars... Anti-business anti-American. As Glenn Beck correctly predicted from day one, Barack Hussein Obama is following the plan of **Cloward & Piven**, two professors at Columbia University . They outlined a plan to socialize America by overwhelming the system* *with government spending and entitlement demands.*

Add up the clues below. Taken individually, they're alarming. Taken as a whole, it is a brilliant, Machiavellian game plan to turn the United States into a Socialist/Marxist state with a permanent majority that desperately needs government for survival. And can be counted on to always vote for even bigger government. Why not? They have no responsibility to pay for it.

Universal Health Care:

The Health Care bill has very little to do with healthcare. It has everything to do with unionizing millions of hospital and healthcare workers as well as adding 15,000 to 20,000 new IRS agents (who will join government employee unions). Obama doesn't care that giving free healthcare to 30 million Americans will add trillions to the national debt. What he does care about is that it cements the dependence of those 30 million voters to Democrats and big government. Who but a socialist revolutionary would pass this reckless spending bill in the middle of a depression?

Cap and Trade:

Like healthcare legislation having nothing to do with healthcare, Cap and Trade has nothing to do with global warming. It has everything to do with redistribution of income, government control of the economy, and a criminal payoff to Obama's biggest contributors. Those powerful and wealthy unions and contributors (like GE, which owns NBC, MSNBC and CNBC) can then be counted on to support everything Obama wants. They will kick-back hundreds of millions of dollars in contributions to Obama and the Democratic Party to keep them in power. The bonus is that all the new taxes on Americans with bigger cars, bigger homes and businesses helps Obama spread the wealth around.

Making Puerto Rico a state:

Who's asking for a 51st state? Who's asking for millions of new welfare recipients and government entitlement addicts in the middle of a depression? Certainly not American taxpayers! But this has been Barack Hussein Obama's plan all along. His goal is to add two new Democrat senators, five Democrat congressmen and a million loyal Democratic voters who are dependent on big government.

(This will tip the balance of those living off the government to more than those who must pay for it; and we're done for.)

Legalize 12 million illegal Mexican immigrants:

Just giving these 12 million potential new citizens free healthcare alone could overwhelm the system and bankrupt America . But it adds 12 million reliable new Democrat voters who can be counted on to support big government. Add another few trillion dollars in welfare, aid to dependent children, food stamps, free medical, education, tax credits for the poor, and eventually Social Security. (see note above re: Puerto Rico)

Stimulus and bailouts

Where did all that money go? It went to Democrat contributors, organizations (ACORN), and unions -- including billions of dollars to save or create jobs of government employees across the country. It went to save GM and Chrysler so that their employees could keep paying union dues. It went to AIG so that Goldman Sachs could be bailed out (after giving Obama almost $1 million in contributions). A staggering $125 billion went to teachers (thereby protecting their union dues).

All those public employees will vote loyally Democrat to protect their bloated salaries and pensions that are bankrupting America . The country goes broke, future generations face a bleak future, but Obama, the Democrat Party, government, and the unions grow more powerful.

The ends justify the means. Raise taxes on small business owners, high-income earners, and job creators. Put the entire burden on only the top

20 percent of taxpayers, redistribute the income, punish success, and reward those who did nothing to deserve it (except vote for Obama).

Reagan wanted to dramatically cut taxes in order to starve the government. Barack Obama wants to dramatically raise taxes to starve his political opposition. With the acts outlined above, Barack Hussein Obama and his regime have created a vast and rapidly expanding constituency of voters dependent on big government; a vast privileged class of public employees who work for big government; and a government dedicated to destroying capitalism and installing themselves as socialist rulers by overwhelming the system.

Add it up and you've got the perfect Marxist scheme all devised by my Columbia University college classmate Barack Hussein Obama using the Cloward-Piven Strategy.

Last point: think about what this designed rule of the rabble will do to anyone successful and everyone receiving this is. What will your lives

*be like under Communism? The time to fight
this abomination is now.*

*

You may or may not agree with Mr. Root's
above provocative pronouncements, but it is
certainly food for thought. History has shown us
many examples of societies that were led by
men with rather shadowy philosophies to a
place the majority of our democracy decries. It
should perhaps make us wary enough to think
about such things. The security of this nation's
cherished democratic ideals is put at risk when
we embrace or are apathetic about political
moves that threaten our freedom and liberty.

Without question, helping those who truly need
our help is necessary, but there must be an
oversight system put into place to preclude
fraud, waste, and incompetence. We have the
technology, if not in the federal government, in
the private sector to create a tight and secure
oversight system.

In our current security climate, one of the most
important goals of this government should be a

National Security System second to none.
Without this viable entity the other priorities
lose some of their vitality... Keep America safe,
Mr. President, by any and all means. Keep away
the dragons that would slay our democratic
principles laid out in the Constitution of the
United State.

3) The Economy

How does Joe Public see the United States economy?

When I was in college many years ago, My Economics professor was dynamic and obviously knew his subject very well. The problem for me was that he spent quite a lot of time on historical people and theory, used complex terms to explain things. He was for me almost too scientific in his approach to teaching Economics. After all, I was just out of the US Navy and still had a brain that operated on the KISS principle (Keep It Simple Stupid), a country boy trying hard to grasp some fundamental principals that came with higher education.

Aside from the more or less traditional definition of Economics that it is a branch of knowledge that is concerned with the production, consumption, and transfer of wealth and the condition of a region or group as regards material prosperity, I believe it can still be too esoteric for some to basically understand. So, bear with me for a moment as I try to explain Economics in my homespun way…for me, as well as the reader…hopefully not insulting your intelligence.

A high school lad comes home from school all confused about one of his teachers references to Economics. The young man at the dinner table raises his red flag about the meaning of Economics. His father finally thinks of a way to describe what he believes the word means to him.

"Son, let's look at Economics from this line of thinking… A young man, a member of a farming family, has just graduated college and he has this idea running loose in his head, let's say it's an idea that deals with an easy method to extract milk from the cows on their farm, in lieu of the old one-on-one bucket and stool way. The young man works for days, weeks, months, and comes up with an intricate system involving tubes, electronics, mechanics of one sort or

another, and puts his plan through testing. He needs to make some modifications but his system works. He is delighted because this means that now more milk can be produced more quickly, more efficiently, and it creates an avenue of extra revenue for his family.

"The family is all excited about the young man's ingenuity and the prospect that they can now buy more cows, sell more milk, make and spend more money. Of course, the young man and the family will have to form a company, determine their marketing strategies on selling to other consumers of milk, to stores, to other outlets – in short, a business plan.

"Soon, the family's business is growing by leaps and bounds. New equipment is needed. More cows are purchased. Salesmen are hired. Marketing people are employed. A plant is needed as are offices, with people to handle the various aspects of the business.

"This is Economics at work, son: an individual or individuals creating a product and/or a product enhancer, putting it in the market place

for consumption of customers, and the distribution of wealth, that is, money going from hands to hands.

"Think about it, whether it be a young man and his milk system, or a couple of guys working in their garage on new and better ways to communicate with the world, or clothing people coming up with new apparel for the seasons, or car engineers working on new engines for less consumption of gas... Get the idea? It is all connected. Economics is an engine that drives our nation and our world. Economics is about risk and reward. It is about honesty and integrity, about pricing policies and profit gouging. Economics is more complicated than I'm making it here, but, for most Americans and other countries of the world, the fundamentals are here. We build. We buy and sell. We consume. We pass money through the system. Workers must be paid fairly. An equitable profit must be made. The Economic machine can be damaged with crop destruction, with bloated oil pricing, with too many government regulations and/or involvement... Books are written about Economics, with the fancy terminologies,

historical perspectives, but I believe I've given you the gist of what most everyday working Americans can understand."

Okay, if I've presented a fairly basic idea of Economics, what are the troubling factors of our Economy today, from a political perspective?

Let's start with jobs and income… Obviously, we are not creating enough jobs. Where do the faults lie? If you're expecting me to say the faults lie with our current administration in Washington, D. C., you are correct. That is where I believe the faults lie. It is true that President Obama inherited economic fallout from the Bush administration. Bush was spending much of taxpayer money on the War on Terror and can perhaps in some small way be criticized for Iraq and the apparent misinformation about weapons of mass destruction… I hasten to add that most of the world was given this false (maybe!) information and Mr. Bush was given approval for invading Iraq. The 'maybe' in parenthesis is there because this Joe Public is not totally satisfied with the notion that there were no weapons of mass destruction. None were found, true, but those weapons of mass destruction could have been diverted to Syria or some other Arab nation. Mr. Bush also added some welfare spending on his watch to add to the money drain.

It is my opinion, however, that President Barack Obama and his administration has used up big time the collateral of 'the Bush inheritance'. Mr. Obama has been president for five years and most likely those who are modestly informed on political matters know the statistical data on earnings and job growth. Certainly, job growth is down as are earnings of the American people. I don't like playing with polls and statistics necessarily because, in many cases, polls and statistics can do what one wishes them to do (plus, they at times confuse and confound me). I prefer to say that we all suffered financially after the 2006 housing bubble and with the recession that followed. It would naturally follow that those who received highly questionable mortgages from government sponsored Fannie Mae and Freddie Mac would be the most severely devastated. It was announced in September, 2008, that these two Government Sponsored Enterprises was being placed into conservatorship. The Treasury Secretary at the time said that this action was attributed 'to the inherent conflict and flawed business model embedded in the structure of the GSEs' (Government Sponsored Enterprises). It should be noted that the oversight of these GSEs were governed by democrats.

There was too the marketing by broker houses of those little understood packaged mortgage bundles, combining good paper with bad paper. This further brought the economy down, and large companies went down as well.

Exorbitant amounts of stimulus money (taxpayer money) were used to stop the financial bleeding but in the estimation of many financial experts the stimulus did very little to stem the freefall of our economy… Most likely, the stimulus money went a long way in paying off political favors. Along with these heavy hits to the taxpayers came cumbersome and lethal regulations to the banking industry, precluding housing loans to those who needed them.

More stimulus money later and with the Federal Government under President Obama taking an active role in creative solar and other businesses, the economy took further hits with the failure of many of these new companies.

There are many more events and reasons why our economy is trillions of dollars in debt. We just experienced here in October, 2013, another closing down of government because the congress could not get together on raising the debt limit. Democrats blamed the Republicans. Republicans blamed the Democrats. There was plenty of blame to spread. The Democrats united in their cause to raise the debt limit while the Republicans old-guard and new guard spoke in different tongues.

One group of Republicans (the old-guard) did not want the new-guard raising issues about the Affordable Care Act, euphemistically dubbed ObamaCare, who wanted, if not to totally de-fund it, to at least defer for one year the obligatory sign-up in the rollout period which had already begun. Many people have reported the site for signing up in ObamaCare is malfunctioning or is not working at all, raising even more doubts about the complexities and expense of the Act. A rather large group of Republicans and some Democrats are demanding that Kathleen Sibelius, Secretary of Health and Human Resources resign her post because she is the person responsible for having the Affordable Care Act ready to go… She has indeed had several years to make the Act operational. Nearly one billion tax payer dollars, possibly much more, have been spent just in this rollout phase of ObamaCare.

Many, believe, as do I, that there is indeed enough evidence to show that this act, ObamaCare, will be the most unwieldy and most costly legislation ever amassed in our history as a republic. As previously mentioned, it is very difficult for me to understand Republican Chief Justice John Roberts' deciding vote in approving this law.

Perhaps there's enough given here regarding the economy. There is without doubt so much more that could be said. From my perspective, the current administration under President Barack

Obama is the most inept and patronizing group of politicians we have ever had in these important seats of power. In fact, I have seen some Republican actions that make me feel the same way.

For me, it is like Anon said: "Life is really simple...people insist on making it complicated." Government should do what it is mandated to do by our US Constitution: protect us and our shores, provide for the education of our young people, help the truly poor, needy, and health handicapped with built-in oversight for fraud and manipulation, make laws that make sense for all people, let the individual states in most instances decide what is best for their people, and be the resource for financial assistance in national emergencies. Allow the private sector to create businesses and jobs. Do not play Mom and Pop to our millions of people and give us our liberty and freedom to choose our own courses. Be there when we need you but do not be in our faces in all aspects of our lives. Accept the fact that we can never have a level playing field for all – there will always be the poor, the rich, and those striving for better.

All attempts to take incentive away from our people, to redistribute wealth and create a 'nanny' state, will only bring down our democracy and destroy our union.

This Joe Public was born in Appalachia, knows the ugly face of disease and poverty, and, while I am not among the wealthy I do not envy them their good fortune. I have what I have by hard work, by good luck, and by my faith which I wish to make stronger each day left to me. The sun rises and sets. The moon, the stars, and the planets are in their places. There is order in the universe and in the nine-month period of a child's birth.

Let us put some order in our economy and in the affairs of state.

JOE PUBLIC'S POLITICAL PERSPECTIVE

4) Guns and Gun Control

I do not like guns. I have fished a bit but have never hunted any animal – if we can exclude the female of our species during my younger years. Although the hunt for animals is not among my favorite pastimes I do understand the enjoyment it gives others and the need to keep certain animal populations at a minimum. I hate violence for I have been there, seen that, and I write books about the angry and ugly ways of man. It would not bother me were it possible to assemble all firearms and all weapons of individual and/or mass destruction and eliminate them forever. But, with whatever wisdom I have, it tells me that this is not possible. Where there is evil, greed, and power seekers, there will always be the impulse to defend, to kill or to be killed.

I do not like too much government control and the 2nd Amendment to our US Constitution gives our citizens the right to keep and bear arms. In Supreme Court rulings, citing this Amendment, the states have had their rights upheld to regulate firearms. Some states have stricter regulations than others. It seems more than reasonable to me that states should have very strict regulations governing ownership of firearms – firearm owner data bases with annual renewal mandates, restrictions on the use of certain firearms (military-style assault weapons). Really, how many of us need Soviet Union's AK-47s around to make us happy – at least, that's where they were developed… I'm just not sure our founding fathers had AK-47s in mind when that Amendment was written.

Guns make some people feel more protected in their homes, in some particular types of business travel, and that is understood. I'm not at odds with the 2nd Amendment, just with some of the firearm types that look ominous, ugly, and go rat-a-tat-tat.

What really bothers me is the massacre of school children, movie goers, and people just out for the day shopping…killed by someone sick in the head or playing too darn many terror-filled video games. Can we stop this kind of madness? In today's world, if someone high on Methamphetamine or a person with a 'loose wire' wants a gun, can he/she not get it? What further makes me boil are the demagogues who try to make political hay from tragedies.

As I write this, a student with a semi-automatic hand gun shot a math teacher and two other students on school ground in Sparks, Nevada before the day's classes began. The teacher attempted to intervene as the students were shot. Apparently, the shooter had been previously bullied at the school. The teacher is dead as is the student shooter who turned the gun on himself. The two students, one just out of surgery, are recovering in a hospital. Authorities at this point indicate no shots were fired by police.

Also at this writing, in the early morning hours at a casino on the Las Vegas Strip, a man was denied entrance to a strip club inside a casino. The man opened fire, killed one person and wounded others before being subdued by some of the patrons.

How much more madness is happening around our country and the world that is connected to guns?

We can never stop it all. That is the bitter truth. That is the world we live in today, and, just maybe, the world we have always lived in. The news travels faster these days, not just on the hot ink print of newspapers but on the internet and cell phones. Our geniuses have harnessed so much of life to make our rotations around the Sun so much easier, to make the delivery of messages faster, to get us to our destinations quicker, to enhance our looks, to bring romance and love for speedy pairing and even hastier disconnect. The machines have indeed arrived.

The section deals with guns and gun control. Why not talk about drug users and pushers? The two sort of go together. The hopheads can do their lines and needle puncturing, blow you away with an un-operational brain and go looking for another high within seconds. Drugs and guns are now gods to some of those babies we held and cuddled so many years ago. The school playgrounds are now business offices for the crew cuts and the long hairs.

We talk and we write about these terrible lunacies in our societies and know very little about what to do about them. We have blue and red states. Which is your preference? Look at a political map of the United States for the last four presidential elections – 2000-2004-2008-2012. Look at the red - Republicans. Look at the blue – Democrats. We are in our One Hundred Thirteenth (113th) United States Congress. We have a Democratic President, a Republican-controlled House of Representatives, and a Democratic-controlled senate. Bills originate in the House and go to the Senate for modification.

Why do I mention any of this?

The red states represent a majority of conservative voters, of which I am one. The blue states represent a majority of liberal voters. If you are a free-wheeling type of person – you might want to legalize drugs, might want wealth redistributed, might want to tax the rich, make it easier for illegal aliens to become citizens, might favor abortion, might want entitlements (food stamps, longer unemployment pay-outs, welfare checks for this or that, cradle to grave health care, might want to say that guns kill, et al). If you are pretty much against these goodies, want the private sector to have the most control over our economy, want entrepreneurs to create businesses and jobs, want investment capital revving our economic engine, a strong military, secured borders, a modified private health care system, no abortions except in dire situations, balanced budget and less entitlement spending, might want to say that men kill, not guns, et al.

In my opinion we are seeing a society where anything goes and the ghost of Nero is picking up his fiddle. Am I too harsh? Perhaps a tad, but I am worried for my children and my grandchildren. We are trillions of dollars in debt with no end in sight. The far left seems to prefer socialism to democracy and want to claim the conservative republicans have their heads buried in the sand. Of course, blame works both ways. The conservatives do their fair part in fouling up the system, but it is my belief that history shows us where socialism leads, to civil unrest, to anarchy, lawlessness and disorder, chaos and turmoil, to dictatorship. Guns and weapons of mass destruction do very well in this shadowy landscape.

So, in the end, it will depend how far our citizens want to go with the new entitlement society of President Obama. It is this President, this liberal administration that is leading our country toward a fiscal cliff. Again, we must take care of our citizens who truly need government's help, but we must not let our country be counted among the socialized failures of history. We want our God-given freedom to make our choices and the liberty to enjoy our lives.

The two principal political parties, except for demagoguery on the left side of the aisle, are not so acidly in opposition on Guns and Gun Control because of the 2nd Amendment to the US Constitution. With this fact and a rather strong NRA lobby (National Rifle Association), we can expect some occasional modifications to our federal and state guidelines. Guns are pieces of metal, inactive and harmless shapes, until they are in the hands of man. They then become play things for enjoyment or instruments of death and mayhem.

One note here, I am no authority on the Constitution of the United States but I do know a bit about the seven articles and the twenty-seven amendments – the first ten amendments are called 'The bill of Rights'. I do know it is a document that cannot so easily be interpreted, and that is why we have the various courts and the Supreme Court to make rulings in cases where the need arises. That precious document is always at your fingertips if you have a computer/laptop. It is always a fresh learning experience when I visit and browse the Constitution online. One can get engrossed in its rich and formal text.

5) The Criminal Justice System

We must live by the 'Rule of Law'. Otherwise, our beautiful country becomes a pitiable wasteland.

Do I believe there are inadequacies in our justice system? Absolutely, yes, I do believe that. Let me tell you a true story which is very personal to me and brings me to sadness and anger in the telling...

My Uncle Stanley was a saint of a man. Not too many years separated us although he was a few years older than I. In our youth we played catch and other games of the day. We talked about life the way kids talk about life, in terms of sports, movies, jobs we might want to hold, about death and dying, and about the role of faith in our lives. Uncle Stanley was so much like his father, my maternal grandfather, a man strong of body and character, a man not afraid to show his love and tender side. These two people were the paragons of my youth, so beautiful they were of soul.

Uncle Stanley grew, got married, had a lovely daughter, and saved enough money to buy the service station he had always wanted. He led a simple life of family, faith, and work. He was a happy man.

Closing his service station one night a young man robbed my uncle, led him to the Men's Room, and brutally killed him with three gunshots. The date was April 21, 1978. I can only imagine the last minutes of my uncle's life – seeing, feeling terror, unable to do anything, possibly holding a thread of hope that the young man would lock him in the men's room and be gone with the daily receipts.

The young man was apprehended in short order, confessed, tried, and sentenced to die for his crime. After spending twenty-three years on death row, his sentence delayed with decades of appeals and changing lawyers, a new attorney found something in a legal document -- a typo, some phrase that went counter to jurisprudence

-- and a judge in Nashville, Tennessee overturned the original robbery and murder convictions, and a new trial was ordered. An appellate judge subsequently overturned the Nashville judge's ruling, leaving the robbery conviction intact but allowing a new trial for the murder. The man was offered a plea deal in 2001, life imprisonment with a parole possibility in thirty years, with time served. At the last minute the man turned down the plea deal. In 2009 the man was offered the same plea deal. This time he accepted. Having already served thirty years he was instantly eligible for parole.

Today, some thirty-five years from the date of Uncle Stanley's murder, the killer still breathes and is likely on parole as I write this.

What you cannot see in these words is the anger I feel for the justice system.

Yes, I hear the platitudes of our judges in their robed regalia and the attorneys who look for any loophole they can find to convict or to defend a case. For me it is time to take a long look at lady justice, to perhaps dress her differently, to make sure she speaks with a true and purer voice. It seems to me so often some ludicrous finding derails a case where there is no doubt whatsoever of the criminal's guilt or innocence.

Now, we have DNA and so many forensic lab tools at our disposal to bring most convictions into the realm of 100 % certainty. Can we not re-model our justice system with truth in sentencing, certainly for those criminals who have time and again failed the recidivism test? Can we stop with the plea deals with the exception of the most minor of cases? Can we give the edge to the victim and her/his family in lieu of the criminal? Am I the only person who sees our criminal justice system in disarray?

I am aware that our prisons are overcrowded, that we are releasing early some rather unsavory people back on our streets. Let's take some money from our runaway welfare entitlement train and build more prisons – maybe even on some uninhabited islands.

The very best idea is to immediately get rid of our current Attorney General, Eric H. Holder, Jr. Look, I'm not the brightest light bulb in the room, but this guy is still running on kerosene that dims, fades, and goes out. This guy is really bad for this administration stew – add Nancy Pelosi and Harry Reid and you have ingredients that will poison the nation. Am I too harsh, uncivil? Yeah, but not as much as I would like – there are some really choice words I could use, but I'm trying to stay as gentlemanly as possible…not civil, but gentlemanly. Speaking of civility, that word is still lost on Harry Reid and Nancy Pelosi.

Want to talk 'Fast and Furious'? Do you remember all those guns that went south of the border? Duh! Eric H., he doesn't know anything about that. He doesn't know about those dudes outside the polling places with heavy sticks either… Can someone just inform me? Is this the big 'change' that the glib Mr. Obama promised America? Is that change really a bunch of misfits running our affairs? Okay, I'm ranting and raving! I get that way when I think of the lack of justice for my Uncle Stanley.

How about Jay Carney? There's a real winner, huh? Where did they get this guy? He's supposed to answer questions and his mouth opens but he doesn't say anything. Nobody knows anything about Benghazi, about the IRS targeting 'Tea Party' folks and other conservative dignitaries, about the shenanigans of the old 'quid pro quo' Congress…

Somebody tell me, do these people really work for us, the citizens of the United States of America? If they do, we have to fire them. They are a true disgrace to our noble heritage and to our intelligence, certainly to the little that I have… As I rave, it is not lost on me that other generations have had their bad apples in the barrel of government. But we should be advancing – with all the Scientific and Technological growth. Also, as I rave, we are still a democracy of the people and by the people.

Yes, Barack Obama was re-elected, with thanks to his entitlement and far left constituents. This is democracy speaking through some awful mistake! More years of this President and his

mindless minions and flunkies and we are truly
on a gravel road to perdition. Yes, I know I'm
like a ranting maniac at this moment, but I'm
tired of these nincompoops parading around in
their suits of power and everyone trying to be
subtle and diplomatic in their manners. These
people in this administration are wearing socks
of different colors. They don't know which end
is up. Inept is too polite a word for this group.
They cannot begin to run this country, to
understand the intricacies of government. Okay,
neither do I, nor am I smart enough to really be
writing this book. But I see, I hear, I feel what
these morons are doing to the land of the free,
the land that I love, and I have a right to scream
bloody hell – even if I fall short of brain power.
Others are having their polite soliloquies but
meaning the same things I'm saying.

Right is right. Wrong is wrong. This
administration is most definitely wrong.
Remember the old 'Network' movie? I feel like
shouting out windows: "I'm mad as hell, and
I'm not going to take it anymore!" Hmm, Peter
Finch's character met a bad ending! Guess I

should be less frenetic, but, then, I'm too old to matter.

Sometimes, perspectives are wrong. Sometimes anger and overreaction are wrong. I'm likely wrong to be so uncivil in my discourse but I feel so strongly that this administration is taking us down the wrong roads. Just one question: How did the vote on the 'Affordable Care Act' go in congress? The answer: not a single Republican cast a vote for it. Would you not think that such a 'wonderful' bill would be favored by at least a few Republicans? The bill is not only massive and cumbersome, not to mention un-read and not understood by even those responsible for it and still un-read today and not understood. Any piece of massive legislation written behind closed doors and smoke-filled rooms without consensus cannot be good. Should not the people writing the bills and the citizens of our country understand a bill of such historical significance? Should not the citizens of the US know the particulars of a bill before it is made into law?

I'm just saying!

You may think I have drifted too far from this section's topic, 'The Criminal Justice System', but, really, I believe it is criminal and without justice to write and enact a bill that will drain our treasury and cost our people and their children and grandchildren dearly. There are so many in an accounting position of high rank that say the same thing about this bill. It staggers my pea-brain mind that Obamacare is the law of this land and that it will cost us trillions of taxpayer dollars – just the rollout itself will likely end up costing us billions.

For those who like Obamacare, who want Mom and Pop Government caring for them cradle to grave, good luck with that. You are going down a socialistic road that has the potential to ruin this great country. If those of you who favor this massive piece of junk legislation still have some hopes and dreams, welcome to your new world of entitlement slavery and the socialist state.

To repeat something I said earlier, there are some good elements to this bill, but these elements could be enacted by private legislation. The government should not be choosing for us. The government should not be our masters, knowing better than us what is good for us. Sure, those who are now without health insurance policies were given an apology by President Obama, NOT for his deceptive words, "If you like your insurance plan, you can keep it, period!" The apology was hollow and without any value to those millions who have already lost by the 'would-be' launch of Obama's ACA.

I'm thinking there is no justice being delivered here...

6) Education

Having taught school for a short time I got a feel for the classroom, the kids, and some subtleties for which a teacher cannot always be prepared and/or expecting.

As a young new teacher I hit the proverbial jackpot. With an English major from a fine Pennsylvania college and with a penchant for writing, I was interviewed to replace a revered Greek teacher of 'Advanced Writing'. The gentleman I did not know and he had passed away from some incurable disease. The superintendent who did my interview told me that the kids in the man's classes adored him and that I could be in for a tough adjustment period. When one is young there are few obstacles that can subdue you. I not only got the 'Advanced Writing' teaching position but inherited as well the position of yearbook advisor.

With me I brought to my new positions all the youthful idealism and great ideas that would make my mostly college prep students take to writing like the proverbial duck to water... He says with an overused cliché. There was also with me some humility, timidity, and I felt there was also a great deal of professionalism.

At the start I did not want to disrupt what the former teacher had put into place – with hour-long classes, the students were allowed to write in their journals the last fifteen-twenty minutes of class – there were extemporaneous writing sessions – there were class discussions on writing context, style, and originality. The classes were fun and it took me about six weeks to gain the favor of my four classes, some ninety-six students...so many when they truly wanted to write (this, of course, meant a lot of work for me, grading, commenting in the margins of their themes, etc.).

My teaching took place in a steel city on Lake Erie and I had in my classes the crème de la crème, the best kids as far as potential for higher education. During the day there were a couple of hours to devote to the high school yearbook, working with bright and energetic kids as staff.

My world was reasonably good, except with a wife and kids I could not make ends meet. So, my leaving the classroom was dictated by the economy and some other considerations – bitter cold along the lake in winter and hot and humid in the summer.

One of my inner struggles in teaching was coping with my conflicting doubts. Visiting the Teachers Lounge I could overhear some of my colleagues talking about some of their students, comments like: "I'd like to blend Johnny B into the blackboard. He's an ass-hole" or "Do you have Sue W in your class? She's really got nice boobs." These teachers were likely good qualified people but it was not what I had expected. Some of them used the language of the streets and it took me by surprise. At the time I felt these people were not professional and that perhaps they were taking up space.

Not making ends meet with my teaching salary was another struggle. I felt teachers were not sufficiently compensated; felt that they occupied such important positions, that more money should be spent on these people who were influencing our children.

While I'm no expert on Education, over the years I have come to believe that the powerful NEA (National Education Association) enjoys amazing bureaucratic control over the nation's public school system but I question how much it truly performs for the schools with its size and structure. There is so much money spent on public education year after year with little to show for it. Many ideas that would make education more viable, more competitive, are ignored and passed over. We hear so much about the 'Voucher System' but only about ten states use it. To be fair and balanced, here are 'Proponent Vs Opponent' views on the subject from Wikipedia:

*

Proponents of Vouchers

Proponents assert that school voucher and education tax credit systems promote **free market** competition among both private and public schools. By allowing parents and students to "vote with their feet," they incentivize schools to increase accountability and school performance. Proponents argue that the competition spurred by vouchers and education tax credits increases the quality and efficiencies of both eligible private schools and local public schools, as they both must perpetually improve in order to maintain enrollment caused by the competitive nature of **dollar voting** and the swift accountability that results from increasing **consumer sovereignty** - allowing individuals to control what product or service they prefer to buy as opposed to **bureaucracy.**

The argument that school vouchers increases quality and efficiencies in schools forced to compete is supported by studies such as "When

Schools Compete: The Effects of Vouchers on Florida Public School Achievement" (Manhattan Institute for Policy Research's, 2003), which concluded that public schools located near private schools that were eligible to accept voucher students made significantly more improvements than did similar schools not located near eligible private schools. Stanford's C.M. Hoxby, who has researched the systemic effects of school choice, determined that areas with greater residential school choice have consistently higher test scores at a lower per-pupil cost than areas with very few school districts. Hoxby found that the effects of vouchers in Milwaukee and of charter schools in Arizona and Michigan on nearby public schools forced to compete made greater test score gains than schools not faced with such competition, and that the so-called effect of **cream skimming** did not exist in any of the voucher districts examined. **Hoxby's** research has found that both private and public schools improved through the use of vouchers. Also, similar competition has helped in manufacturing, energy, transportation, and parcel postal (**UPS, FedEx vs. USPS**) sectors of government that have been **socialized** and later opened up to free market competition.

Similarly, it is argued that such competition has helped in higher education, with publically funded universities directly competing with private universities for tuition money provided by the Government, such as the **GI Bill** and the **Pell Grant** in the United States.

The **Foundation for Educational Choice** alleges that a school voucher plan "embodies exactly the same principle as the GI bills that provide for educational benefits to military veterans. The veteran gets a voucher good only for educational expense and he is completely free to choose the school at which he uses it, provided that it satisfies certain standards.

Proponents claim that frequently institutions are forced to operate at higher efficiencies when they are allowed to compete and that any resulting job losses in the public sector would be offset by the increased demand for jobs in the private sector.

Friedrich von Hayek on the privatizing of education:

As has been shown by Professor Milton Friedman (M. Friedman, The role of government in education, 1955), it would now be entirely practicable to defray the costs of general education out of the public purse without maintaining government schools, by giving the parents vouchers covering the cost of education of each child which they could hand over to schools of their choice. It may still be desirable that government directly provide schools in a few isolated communities where the number of children is too small (and the average cost of education therefore too high) for privately run schools. But with respect to the great majority of the population, it would undoubtedly be possible to leave the organization and management of education entirely to private efforts, with the government providing merely the basic finance and ensuring a minimum standard for all schools where the vouchers could be spent.

Other notable supporters include Newark Mayor **Cory Booker**, former Governor of South Carolina **Mark Sanford**, billionaire and American philanthropist **John T. Walton**, Former Mayor of Baltimore **Kurt L. Schmoke**, Former Massachusetts Governor **Mitt Romney** and **John McCain**.

Some proponents of school vouchers, including the Sutherland Institute and many supporters of the Utah voucher effort, see it as a remedy for the negative cultural impact caused by under-performing public schools, which falls disproportionately on demographic minorities. During the run-up to the November referendum election Sutherland issued a controversial publication: Voucher, Vows, & Vexations. Sutherland called the publication an important review of the history of education in Utah while critics just called it revisionist history. Sutherland then released the subsequent companion article in a law journal as part of an academic conference about school choice.

The Friedman **Foundation for Educational Choice**, founded by Milton and Rose Friedman in 1996, is a non-profit organization that promotes universal school vouchers and other forms of school choice. In defense of vouchers, it cites empirical research showing that students who were randomly assigned to receive vouchers had higher academic outcomes than students who applied for vouchers but lost a random lottery and did not receive them; and that vouchers improve academic outcomes at public schools, reduce racial segregation, deliver better services to special education students, and do not drain money from public schools.

Opponents of Vouchers

The main controversy over both school vouchers and education tax credits is that they put public education in direct competition with private education, threatening to reduce and reallocate public school funding to private schools. Proponents of a voucher system are encouraged by private school sector growth as it is their view that private schools are typically more efficient at achieving results at a much lower per pupil cost when compared to public schools. A **CATO Institute** study of public and private school per pupil spending in Phoenix, Los Angeles, D.C., Chicago, New York City, and Houston found that public schools spend 93% more than estimated median private schools. However, much variation exists in private school spending, so an average of how much "less" private schools spend as compared to public schools can be misleading.

Jonathan Kozol, a former public school teacher and prominent public school reform thinker has called vouchers the "single worst, most dangerous idea to have entered education discourse in my adult life." Other public school teachers and teacher unions have also fought against school vouchers. In the United States, public school teacher unions, most notably the **National Education Association** (the largest labor union in the USA), argue against the idea of school vouchers for concern that it would erode educational standards and reduce funding, and that giving money to parents who choose to send their child to a religious or other school is unconstitutional; however, the latter issue has been struck down by the **Supreme Court** case **Zelman v. Simmons-Harris**, which upheld Ohio's voucher plan in a 5-4 ruling. In contrast, the use of public school funding for vouchers to private schools was upheld by the Louisiana Supreme Court in 2013. In its ruling the Louisiana Supreme Court did not declare vouchers unconstitutional; just the use of money earmarked for public schools via the Louisiana Constitution for funding Louisiana's voucher program. The **National Education Association** also points out that access to vouchers is just like "a chance in a lottery" where parents had to have luckiness in order to get a space in this program. Since almost all students and their families would like to choose the best schools, those schools, as a result, quickly reach its maximum capacity number for students that state law permits. The major "unlucky families" then have to compete again to look for some other less preferred and competitive schools or give up searching and go back to their assigned local schools.

It is interesting to note that despite widespread availability of vouchers in some states, very few parents opt for vouchers. The number of Louisiana students eligible for vouchers in 2012 was 380,000, only 5,000 students opted to accept the vouchers in order to "escape" public school.

In 2006, the **United States Department of Education** released a report concluding that average test scores for reading and mathematics, when adjusted for student and school characteristics, tend to be very similar among public schools and private schools. If results were left unadjusted for factors such as race, gender, and free or reduced price lunch program eligibility, private schools performed significantly better than public schools. Other research questions assumptions that large improvements would result from a more comprehensive voucher system.

Given the limited budget for schools, it is claimed that a voucher system would weaken public schools while at the same time not necessarily providing enough money for people to attend **private schools**. 76% of the money handed out for Arizona's voucher program has gone to children already in private schools.

Some sources claim that public schools' higher per pupil spending is due to having a higher proportion of students with behavioral, physical and emotional problems. They argue that some, if not all, of the cost difference between public and private schools comes from a process known as **cream skimming**—selecting only those students that belong to a preferred economic, religious, or ethnic group—rather than from differences in administration.

In the United States, public schools must by law accept any student regardless of race, gender, religion, disability, etc. Thus, it has been argued that a voucher system would lead students who do not belong to a preferred religious or ethnic group, or those with disabilities, to become concentrated within the public school system. Of the ten state-run voucher programs in the United States at the beginning of 2011, however, four targeted low-income students, two targeted students in failing schools, and six targeted students with special needs. (Note that Louisiana ran a single program targeting all three groups.)

Another argument against the implementation of a school voucher system is its lack of accountability to the taxpayer. In many states, members of a community's board of education are elected by voters. Similarly, a school budget faces a referendum. Meetings of the Board of Education must be announced in advance, and members of the public are permitted to voice their concerns directly to board members. Although vouchers may be used in private and religious schools, taxpayers are not able to vote on budgetary issues, elect members of the board or even attend board meetings. **Kevin Welner** points out that vouchers funded through a convoluted tax credit system—a policy he calls "Neovouchers"—present additional accountability concerns. With neovoucher systems, a taxpayer owing money to the state instead donates that money to a private, nonprofit organization. That organization then bundles donations and gives them to parents as vouchers to be used for private school tuition.

The state then steps in and forgives (through a tax credit) some or all of the taxes that the donor has given to the organization. While conventional tax credit systems are structured to treat all private school participants equally, neovoucher systems effectively delegate to individual private taxpayers (those owing money to the state) the power to decide which private schools will benefit.

An example of lack of accountability is the voucher situation in Louisiana. In 2012, Louisiana State Superintendent of Education John White selected private schools to receive vouchers then attempted to fabricate criteria (including site visits) after schools had already received approval letters. One school of note, New Living Word in Ruston, Louisiana, did not have sufficient facilities for the over-300 students White and the state board of education had approved. Following a voucher audit in 2013, New Living Word had overcharged the state $395,000. White referred to the incident as a "lone substantive issue." However, most voucher schools did not undergo a complete audit for not having a separate checking account for state voucher money.

Some **libertarians** in the U.S. object to vouchers on the grounds that granting government money, even indirectly, to private and religious schools will inevitably lead to increased governmental control over non-government education, and possibly over the teachings of the sponsoring religious group (most often a church). Some individuals who oppose vouchers on these grounds call for the abolition of all state sponsorship of education. The Alliance for the Separation of School & State opposes education vouchers on the grounds that "if vouchers become commonplace, private and religious schools will become more and more like public schools." Moreover, they suggest that if it is wrong in principle for the government to tax in order to fund public education, then one should not accept any portion of the ill-gotten money to fund private education.

According to Susanne Wiborg, an expert on comparative education, Sweden's voucher system introduced in 1992 has "augmented social and ethnic segregation, particularly in relation to schools in deprived areas."

Tax-credit scholarships which are in most part disbursed to current private school students or to families which made substantial donations to the scholarship fund, rather than to low-income students attempting to escape from failing schools, amount to nothing more than a mechanism to use public funds in the form of foregone taxes to support private, often religiously based, private schools.

*

You can pick the arguments you like. I prefer those that give the highest priority to learning. We talk so much about the importance of education but it seems we just keep pumping money into a system that does not give us a real bang for our bucks. And, of course, the NEA will complain about funding other possibly worthwhile projects…it's the largest union in the United States.

What I think we need is a competitive atmosphere for learning, creating an environment where the poorer performing schools have to close their doors and the students have to attend the achieving schools that demand more. Whether that successful student goes by voucher to a private school or by voucher to a home schooling situation or charter schools designed for those who need the special needs.

We have good teachers in place, some who are being stifled by an archaic system governed by union leaders. These good teachers are alongside the not so good teachers, and perhaps that's the way it must always be. At the very least, though, we must produce the brightest kids on the planet to deal with some of our social and technological problems. The dividends will be there many times over if we can force ourselves to try some new ways of mining the wisdom from some of our bright youngsters, kids who are eager to learn but do not want the old failed, stale, uninteresting ways of learning. We need highly motivated teachers with exciting techniques to teach the important concepts of the new millennium. And, we need to pay them well.

Education is the key to our future, in our public/private schools and in our colleges and universities. It must be education without indoctrination, liberal or conservative, fact-based, fair and balanced with no hints of bias. If you are of the liberal persuasion, my words will no doubt sound hollow and meaningless, without substance. It is said that a conservative will not change the mind of a liberal, and a liberal will not change the mind of a conservative. It truly amazes me that the two minds can at times be polar opposites.

How can I feel so strongly in my beliefs and feelings? How can I see things so very differently? I'm not a wealthy man. I have no envy of the rich – chances are they got their wealth 'the old fashioned way' and earned it. Many of those rich folks care about the less fortunate and are charitable. They believe, as I do, that we need to provide for those who truly need our help. Many such programs are already in place. We can and should do more, but with strong oversight components.

'The Machines' (the digital age) have brought exciting new dimensions to education. Big kids and little kids love the 'machines' and perhaps at times too much. Competing with the school computers we have small electronic game devices which show people killing people with automatic assault rifles and hand machine guns, bombs bursting, people lying in pools of blood. Okay, I played Cowboys and Indians as a kid with toy six shooters, went 'bang bang' and got a little exercise. Yes, that was yesterday. Today's today!

What particularly frightens me about these electronic games is the frequency of use. Is damage being done to the kid's wiring? Is some sort of psychological harm being done? Can this game killing somehow get ingrained in the kid's mind? Are these electronic games replacing the good aspects of exercising, playing in the park, riding the bicycle? Yes, it's a new generation and knowledge is doubling so fast it's hard for this old mind to keep up. But I still worry and hope the professionals are doing their studies and getting good data.

In the end one can only hope that education is also taking place in the home as well as at school. We can hope but we know that for so many kids in broken homes, in state-run institutions, in public housing, they will stay in the shadows for most of their lives, afraid to venture too far into the light, living a solitary life. Others will come out of those shadows with anger and hatred in their hearts to become whatever it is they are to become. Education will be too late for some of our kids. They will grow into people of the streets, alley dwellers, prostitutes, robbers, killers, and society will hate them, never caring, never mindful that once they were children that should have been loved.

You will see them wandering down the streets, down the halls of an old school building that should have been torn down years ago, without a smile, without any hint of feeling any kind of emotion – automatons that are lost forever to the human race.

If not education, what? Take some of the fraud billions wasted in Obama's entitlement money and build healthy recreation centers for kids with good responsible people to run them, people who came from where the kids came but somehow beat the averages. President Obama, you were once a 'Community Organizer' – let's see you work some magic. Let's save those we can, whatever it takes.

JOE PUBLIC'S POLITICAL PERSPECTIVE

7) Capitalism and the Free Enterprise System

What does this section title mean to you? Of course, I'm writing the book, so what does it mean to me? Let me give it a shot...

A brother and sister have depleted their monthly allowance and there's a movie they want to see at the local theater. They talk over an idea and decide to open a lemonade stand out on the edge of their front lawn where the sidewalk stands. They haul an old folding table from the basement out to the lawn's edge, design and make a clever 'Lemonade for Sale' sign. Mom pitches in and makes up several gallons of her tasty lemonade and the kids are ready to open for business. It's a warm summer day and some neighbors and strangers pass by and buy a cool drink for ten cents a cup. The kids make enough money for their movie, but, more importantly, an idea is formed in their heads. Mom and Dad will help to foster that idea for the future.

A man doesn't like working in a company environment, likes playing with ideas and ways to make a good living on his own. He stumbles on the idea of a Styrofoam glass to hold hot liquids like coffee and tea. After he puts his thoughts down, configures on paper his Styrofoam glass, he researches the manufacturing and marketing aspects of his idea. He visits several people who have experience and the willingness to help him. After months pass the man is ready to protect his idea with government documentation that states this idea, this product, is his and his alone. The man will go on to become a millionaire with his Styrofoam cup.

The boy and the girl, the man, have experienced America's Free Enterprise System – Capitalism at work. They have experienced the freedom, the liberty, to expand their dreams into reality. Of course, there are a few government regulations with which to deal, but you get my simplistic example of Capitalism and the Free Enterprise System.

We live in a country where thoughts can be big, where risk and reward are the factors that determine success and failure, where the individual is free to take those risks in chasing her/his dreams, where one can work as hard or as little as they wish.

We have people in the United States like the man with the Styrofoam cup, who worked hard on an idea that became real and beneficial to an entire nation. With his idea, he created manufacturing jobs, sales jobs, and he became very wealthy.

Should we envy this man? Should we want to take a portion of what this man has earned and redistribute it to people who are poor, infirm, and cannot truly make a living on their own? That is already happening in a multitude of programs in existence, like Medicare for retirees, Medicaid for the indigent and sick. We do have 'safety nets' for our people who, through no fault of their own (seniors, handicapped, low IQs, homeless) need government help. We provide those benefits today as I write this, and it costs billions of dollars to the taxpayers of this country. The wealthy pick up the biggest part of the tab and the middle class pick up the rest.

Now the tirade…

Now we have a government that wants to change a lot of our America, make it look a lot like other nations of the world who have socialism. They want to redistribute more of the money hard working people are making and give it to the poor --- I'm not a statistical guy, but check the statistics for the poor today: most of them have cars, televisions, places to live, and those I'm talking about have jobs. We have others classified as poor who can make more money from what they rake in on welfare than working – there is no incentive to work. I'm not being mean-spirited here – I'm retired, have one home and one car, live on a fixed income, and do have just a little money in reserve for emergencies. The people who truly need our help should get it but billions of dollars of taxpayer money is being doled out on fraudulent claims, going to people to have made it a way of life to take from the government (i. e., the group of earners, the taxpayers).

The administration we now have running our country wants to redistribute wealth, wants to build a constituency of voters who will keep them forever in power. After all, when you don't have to work, can stay home and make more than if you were working, why not? That is part of what this Obama administration is building in our country: dependency, lack of incentive, people against people environment, suspicion, doubt – all the precursors for a dark-age society.

President Barack Obama has one precious gift and he uses it to infect minds from the truth: the gift of gab…he is an excellent speaker, a man who I'm sure believes just about all the words that come from his mouth. He very likely believes redistribution is right, that Obamacare is right, that the people who are in his administration are right. How else can one explain his total denial of personal responsibility on any matter? The man knows one thing, campaigning, and that is what he does. He does not govern, and those in his seats of power are so inept as to make them Keystone Kops. If one can possibly think Obama believes in our Free Enterprise System, please drink some more kool-aid.

Has anyone heard him claim responsibility for Benghazi? Has anyone heard him talk about his lack of leadership in Libya, Syria, Iran, Iraq, on and on?

Here at home, has he laid blame at the woman who directs Health and Human Resources, the woman who had three plus years to get Obamacare ready for rollout? No. This is a rollout that has cost the American taxpayer one billion dollars and counting – JUST the rollout. Still at home, has he laid blame on anyone at the IRS for targeting Republican taxpayers? No. Has he laid blame on Attorney General Eric Holder or any of his people for the thousands of guns that went into Mexico? No. He only says that the problems will be fixed and those who have caused problems will be held responsible.

He is a great speaker, a man of charm, but does he often say anything of great import?

After his re-election by his faithful liberal buddies, the folks who are on his welfare dole, or those who really don't much care about what is going on in the country, the man appears to have become even more divisive, more critical of his conservative enemies in congress, otherwise the man who keeps promising us change and hope. We have seen the 'change' and it is not to this Joe Public very pretty. The hope, as I see it, is a resignation party for Obama and a congressional slate cleaning... This statement is made knowing that we do have some devoted servants for 'We The People', those who are really trying to do what is right for our country and to keep those ideals we hold dear.

Our Free Enterprise System is in many ways under attack by the current administration and there appears to be a growing apathy, dare I say, a capitulation to big government running our businesses and our lives. Our Middle Class is hurting. We need investment capital and entrepreneurs in the private sector to provide jobs, to give workers a chance to enjoy the perks of their labor, advancements, pay raises, all parts of the American Dream.

After leaving teaching, I became a small part of that American Dream. For twenty-odd years I worked in the school publishing business, finally made it into marketing and management level jobs, to ultimately reach a National Management position – much of the success I enjoyed was just good luck, good friends in the right places, and some long hours. After publishing, I was a small business owner, and this was perhaps the happier days of my business life. There is nothing more gratifying than knowing that my efforts contributed to a good home, good car, family vacations, and good friends. Mistakes, I made my share. Successes were mine as well.

All in all the United States is truly the land of the free. Free people can go where their talents and their will can take them. Some of us for one viable reason or another cannot make it, so those of us who can make it need to help them… But, there is one caveat: we must be true to our budgets and to our goals. This, our government must do as well.

Some minor modifications might come along to further enrich our Free Enterprise System. That is fine by me. Just give me my freedom to choose what it is I wish to do. Just give me the right to believe in my God without taking old traditions away for the sake of a few non-believers. Those few non-believers have a right to their beliefs, of course. That is the American way -- just do not defile or tread on the beliefs of the majority.

JOE PUBLIC'S POLITICAL PERSPECTIVE

8) The War on Terror and Islam – Reflections

So much of the history of mankind has been tied to religion and religious wars…ever since Adam and Eve left the Garden of Eden and grew all those tribes. The Bible tells us of all the 'begats' and all the feuding and fighting in the 'Old' and 'New' Testament. I've read some in the Bible, but I'm not setting myself up as an expert – far from it. It is certainly a Best Seller and the most widely distributed book in the world. A lovely book with many wonderful chapters and verses, it is many times open for interpretation, not always understood because of the language in which it is written.

Basically, what I get from the Bible is that God (in Genesis) took seven days to separate the firmament from the sea and to create all living things. Adam and Eve sinned and were banished from the Garden of Eden. Cain's heart was filled with evil and he killed Abel who was favored by God. Abel was a shepherd and his blood sacrifices pleased God more than the leftover crop sacrifices of Cain the farmer (not given with a willing heart). After all the 'begats' the tribes spread to different regions. There were wars. There were priests. There were kings. There were prophets. There was Moses who finally freed his people from the Pharaoh in Egypt, separated the Red Sea to escape the Egyptian soldiers, and wandered for years across the desert until his people became vile and wicked. Moses went up to Mount Sinai, spent many days and returned with the Ten Commandments, only to find his people living in sin. At Moses death, Joshua led the Israelites in the conquering of Canaan. There were many more wars in the Old Testament, interfacing with some beautiful chapters and verses like Psalms, Proverbs, Ecclesiastes, and The Song of Solomon…lovely poetic verses that can speak to today as well as to those ancient days.

A believer, I have my faith and I am still confused about the 'begats' and the tribes, but the most striking part for me about the Old

Testament are all the battles that were fought…seems some things do not change…

Today we fight a war on terror with an enemy like we've never known, an enemy that wraps itself in the cloth of Islam and claims 'Jihad' as their battle cry – a Holy War to defend or spread their beliefs. The scary ingredient in this war is the invisible nature of the enemy – they wear no uniforms to announce their coming and they contradict all that is inviolable in modern warfare, and they WANT to kill us…apparently there are virgins awaiting their arrival in their heaven so their own deaths mean little or nothing to them.

This enemy is a relatively small part of Islam, a monotheistic religion with Abraham as its center. Abraham along with Adam, Noah, Moses, Jesus, and Mohammad are considered prophets in the Islam religion, with Mohammad considered the last prophet of God. Adherents of the Islam faith are called Muslims and their beliefs are articulated through a book called the Qur'an…considered by followers as the verbatim word of God. Islam is the second largest and one of the fastest growing religions in the world, its numbers well over 1.5 billion (23% of the world's population)... Christianity is the largest religion.

Most Muslims are of two denominations, the Sunni (75-90%) and Shia (10-20%) and sizable minorities of the Islam religion are found throughout the world. Muslims believe the purpose of their existence is to love and serve God. For some extremists, their purposes are beheadings, blowing up buildings, killing many innocent people...all in the name of their God.

So, there are within the Islam religion the enemies who want to kill us, radical and extreme Muslims who isolate portions of the Qur'an to validate their terrorism. It should be assumed that this section does not cast any unfavorable opinions on an otherwise honorable and noble religion. Religious freedom is a given. To kill in the name of a religion that professes love and service to God is sacrilege of the first order.

Someone recently said, and I paraphrase, "I found out all I wanted to know about Islam after 9/11." While I understand the sentiment, I would not lump terrorist thugs into a large religion to arrive at my understanding of something as evil as 9/11. The actions on 9/11 and other acts of terror by these radical Muslims are evil in the purest sense of the word and the perpetrators deserve our hatred. Our government must use all its energy to find and destroy them…by any means. If torturing a captured terrorist to gain useful information that would result in saving American lives, then I would use torture as a last resort to get that data.

One of the largest non-Arab Muslim countries is Iran. This country perhaps represents the biggest threat in the Middle East, with their growing nuclear capabilities and their strong hatred for Israel – the United States' most solid and true ally in the area. Iran has made it no secret that they wish to destroy this great ally of the US.

The nation of Iran is manipulative and duplicitous and it is my fear (and others' fears) that this Obama administration has not and is not using a big enough 'stick' in dealing with this adversary. Surely, Iran is responsible for much of the unrest in the Middle East – supplying arms and military support to other factions in the region.

Just recently a six-month agreement was reached with Iran regarding their nuclear build-up, halting their current capacities, freezing key parts of their or scaling back their nuclear infrastructure. The agreement is supposedly a first step, stopping the building of new centrifuge installations – those plants where uranium is enriched – and minimizing the levels of enrichment. This agreement seems in reality a very weak trade-off. In fact, many believe the Iranians will do little to curb their appetite for a nuclear bomb. Many believe that, instead of lessening some of the sanctions placed on Iran previously, more sanctions should have been added as well as a demand that all Iranian nuclear ambitions be abolished.

As might be too obvious I am not a scientist, nuclear expert, or a specialist in Middle East matters, but it does seem to me and my conservative mindset that the United States is now not considered in many parts of the world the super power that we once were. Bullies find it easy to harass and do damage to those who show weakness. Even as a bystander, I see weakness in the way our government is handling foreign affairs.

There is one thing that seems abundantly clear to me as regards Muslims coming to live in our land of the free. The United States cannot expect other countries to adopt our system of government, our rites of religion, our 'salad bowl' culture, but we should be able to expect the people who come to our shores for a new life to assimilate and become one with us. That includes Muslims of the Islam faith.

Our country, in its desire to favor different government regimes in foreign lands, made some mistakes in the past, gave aid and arms to those we felt it in our best interest to do so, caused certain factions to hate us enough to kill us, but there is one undeniable truth that trumps all other considerations. We have given generously from our treasury to countries facing disasters and turmoil. I know of no other nation than the United States that has been so noble in giving billions and billions of dollars to help countries in need… Some of these countries now cast blame and insult us while still taking our dollars and aiding in the killing of our citizens.

Like an individual, no nation is perfect, but we stand as close to that ideal as any country I know. We cannot wave a magic wand and make the world a better place. People must want freedom and liberty enough to see beyond their apathy and prejudices. We have fought our wars and we now fight a new enemy, the Muslim Fanatics and Terrorism. There is nothing more important than protecting our people and our shores.

While it is fundamental to our nature to want a free world republic, we must be realistic in facing the limitations of the United Nations. It has become dysfunctional and counter-productive. We know and can predict the actions of our adversaries in that organization.

We give them voice to spew their demands and vitriol and spend so much of our money in doing so.

When oceans separate us, when cultures clash, when speech can be misunderstood, when envy and hatred prevail, how can we ever expect to create a new world order? The answer is, we cannot. Certainly, history teaches us that. No one can tell another who it is he/she should confirm in friendship. With all of us in different mindsets, different levels of understanding, how is it possible to unite us all? When minority groups and those who care to eat at the public trough can sway the steerage of a nation, where is a democracy to go?

For this 'Joe Public', we must pay attention to the vast majority of our people, the cries of the 'Tea Party' folks, those who still believe their tears and the cries from their souls enough to keep their faith in God. For those who want their socialism, communism, let them go to those countries that can appease them. Change must come and change is good, but not for just those who fight the Constitutional fundamentals sacred to most of us.

The 'Machines' have arrived to double our knowledge so quickly, to provide us with games to play and social networks to span the oceans. Have the machines made it too easy for us to forget some of our basic tenets and truths? The machines can do wonders for learning and teaching, but should there not be rules of use in the personal arena? Are the machines making it easier for our Muslim Fanatics, the terrorists, to plan their evil?

In short, must we not put priority on applying regulations to keep evil away? Democracy and Freedom is all important to me but it does not mean we cannot safeguard our digital wizardry with some good old common sense.

9) Religion and Faith

Churches are beautiful and comforting to so many. My early years of life serve up Southern Baptist memories of Sunday church meetings, Wednesday prayer meeting services, summer Bible Schools. The religion of my youth is altered today in the twilight years. As a little boy I was made to believe I was 'a sinner in the hands of an angry God'. When the pastor at the end of his sermon asked the congregation to stand and sing hymns during the altar call, the emotional frenzy inside my body made me weak. I felt like a really bad little boy when, in actuality, I was a good lad…of course, you can only take my word for that. At the early age of eight, I accepted Jesus as my savior and was baptized. Through elementary, junior, and senior high school I tried very hard not to speak bad words or do bad things. For the most part I succeeded.

Today, my faith is still there – though I wish it to be stronger. I don't go to church on Sundays anymore and I find my God in the natural beauty in the world, the oceans, the mountains, the deserts, the sun, moon, and stars. My humility is intact (with the possible exception of this book) and I try to treat people with kindness and respect. I could possibly be mistaken for an agnostic, but there are too many ways to show God's handiwork that make me a believer: those natural things mentioned above but the clincher for me is that nine-month cycle of birth, that meticulous and orderly pattern of life formation.

Faith is of course intangible, but I feel it in so many ways. My soul reminds me that there is God when I read a good book or see a sad movie and tears come. Faith is not something you can force or tell someone to have. Faith is something you must have when you are thinking of the chicken and egg conundrum, infinity, or the sound of a tree falling in the forest when no one is around to hear it fall. Faith can be a refuge when a loved one departs or at contemplation of departure. Faith can be strong or weak.

When I'm around people of strong faith who wish to prevail upon me to go to church, to become more involved in church activities, I tell them that I've been there, done that. My wife and I once were very active in our church but saw the ugly face of politics come to the house of worship – pitting deacons against elders against pastor. My revelation here does not mean anything negative against church-going…it is merely a personal decision for my wife and me. On occasion we still go, and we believe that the church provides a needed spiritual service.

Can I put a name on my religion? I'm still a protestant. I believe Jesus is a man who lived among us and gave us some beautiful words by which to live. So far as I can know, Jesus was without sin and **was** the Son of God. I believe that he died for the sins of us all. I believe, hope, pray, have faith that there is another dimension beyond this life. I believe that the bible is a big part of our recorded history – Old and New Testaments. I also believe that there are many interpretations that one can make from the Bible.

It is sometimes easier for me to say what it is I don't necessarily believe when it comes to the divide of Religion and Non-Believers. This whole thing had a beginning – the earth/universe had a beginning. Otherwise, I'm lost in the non-solvable mystery of infinity. Primarily, because of the miracle of birth, I cannot believe that we exist as the result of a 'Big Bang'. I do believe in Science and all that science has given our lives…science and technology (good and bad). But I have lived and I will die. It is my wish to have faith that there is another realm in which I may go after death that will eliminate the negatives of this life.

If a Non-Believer – an Atheist – believes me to be foolish in my belief and faith, I would only counter by saying that it is he/she that displays an arrogance and impudence on the subject. While no one can say what happens after death to the spirit that leaves the body, it will be my belief and faith that that unseen part of me – my spirit – goes on to exist in a place called heaven, or, to perhaps live again in this dimension by returning in another form.

All cultures throughout the world have their belief systems. They either believe we die and it's all over or they believe in whatever denomination that there is life after death. It goes without my saying that all people have a right to their beliefs. I respect the religious beliefs of others, except for those factions that want to kill me and destroy my country. There is one other minor exception for me… Some atheists have a way of irritating me, with their dogmatic certainty that there is nothing after death. They can give us scientific theory and their own self-proclaimed wisdom which I find arrogance of the highest order. Could they not simply claim agnosticism? What wisdom do they hold claim that they can state with a definite air that there is but darkness after death?

It is my opinion that should people want to have relative peace among their peer groups they should likely not discuss politics and religion.

I'm left with one salient observation. There are billions of people in the world following either Abrahamic religion, Indian religion, or East Asian religion. The numbers break down this way: Abrahamic religion (chronologically, Judaism, Christianity, and Islam) is followed by 54% of the world's population – 3.8 billion people; Indian and East Asian religion are followed by 30% of the world's population; 16% of the world's population follow no organized religion. What do these facts and all the history tell me? 84% of the people in the world carry with them Faith. This Faith came down through the ages, important and viable enough for the great majority of mankind to believe in something other than darkness.

It would seem to me important that we believe in ourselves and something far greater than ourselves. Whether we are monotheistic (Abrahamic religion) in our beliefs or Dharmic (Indian religion) or Taoist (East Asian religion), we believe not only in ourselves but in something remarkable and of great significance in our lives. While my Faith has at times been tenuous, while I still stumble at times, I will keep my Faith and believe that a new adventure begins for me at my earthly passing.

10) The Secular Mind-set

Some would have us believe that the 'secular progressive' folks are behind the many attempts to take our God away, to make the world an 'anything goes' kind of world. Some influential people and corporations are busy as I write trying to influence the minds of our youth and adults that all this business about religion, Christmas, and the Easter bunny is all just a bunch of foolishness. You see it every year at Christmas time when these secular folks don't want us to say 'Merry Christmas' or even go shopping for a 'Christmas Tree' – they want 'Happy Holidays' (which is fine because I say that along with my 'Merry Christmas') or 'Holiday Tree'. In this year of 2013 there are some schools in our country that do not want our kids singing Christmas Carols in their choral groups and/or in their Yule time school performances.

Why is it that the majority which is supposed to rule in our country do not become more vocal when this government holiday is mocked by this kind of behavior? Why is that 'political correctness' has reached a critical point of absurdity in this land of the free? There is no wish on my part and I dare say on the majority's part to deny any religious group their celebratory rites. Why this stupid 'war on Christmas' by the secular minority? After all, Christmas is a government holiday. Jesus was a man who lived among the people and gave us guiding principles by which to live, a man who many in our religious communities believe was the Son of God. If he was just a man among us, it would still be enough to honor him for his faith, his spirit, and his words – not so unlike we do with another good man, Martin Luther King.

Many progressive activists or secularists often rally around the First Amendment to the United States Constitution which concerns itself with freedom of speech, freedom of the press, religious freedom, freedom of assembly, and right to petition. It seems that within any legal framework there could be some loopholes for some to find some judicial argument. Chief Justice Waite wrote in 'Reynolds v. United States in 1878' that "Freedom of religion means freedom to hold an opinion or belief, but not to take action in violation of social duties or subversive to good order." So far as I know, efforts to change that meaning have failed.

Someone once said: "It's better to be thought stupid than to open your mouth and prove it." I'm not so thoroughly knowledgeable of the seven articles and twenty-seven amendments of the United States Constitution to stay too long on the subject. I'm acquainted more with certain amendments than with others. I know how an amendment must be presented and how it must be ratified. It's my understanding that thirty-three amendments have been considered over the years. Of those, twenty-seven have prevailed – some would say twenty-six since the twenty-first amendment overhauled the eighteenth amendment. I've read through the constitution and admit that much of its 'rich text' loses me, but it's always there on our electronic devices if we care to take a look. It might lose me in spots but the United States Constitution is one of the most dynamic documents in the world's history, and our government leaders should follow it closely.

I'm a conservative-thinking person and I remember my days of liberal youth when I cared very little about the left, far-left, right, far-right. Other than knowing the president holding office and some television network news images I was more interested in finding myself than sorting through the affairs of a nation. In aging, I've become more informed about the political schisms. That is, I've watched newscasts, cable TV pundits and 'no spin' programs, read some political books of both persuasions, and, from the minimal brain power endowed by my southern roots, I've come to my personal observations of what is right and what is wrong.

Whether the digital age with its distractions and games, whether the corporate conglomerates with their money and influence, whether the decline of families, the absence of a father and/or mother, the rise of permissiveness, the easy access to drugs, whether the supersonic jets and new ways of fighting wars, whatever the multitude of causes, brash and anything-goes secularism is now firmly entrenched in our country. From where I sit the nation I love is getting uglier with each passing day.

Christianity is taking a back seat to the rampant rise of Secularism, from the movies coming out of Hollywood, from the TV shows which have put new meaning to ribald behavior, from the electronic games that allow the players to kill and thrill at the sight of blood pools. Students and teachers can harass, fight in their classrooms and on school buses. Computers are used as weapons with impunity against those we don't like and can lead to teens killing themselves. One is reluctant to mention God and faith for fear of receiving ridicule or worse.

Okay, sure, we don't have to watch the movies, the TV shows. We can only use computers for educational purposes, for games of Solitaire and Hearts. We can find ways to ignore the secular onslaught. Yes, we can ignore but we give up little pieces of ourselves in the acceptance of anything-goes. The world turns with us all taking the ride, the secular progressives and those of us who have the majority in this country. Sure, we are living side by side so what's the big deal? I guess it all comes to this point: what kind of life do you want for your children and grandchildren? Keep fun on the board, even a wee bit of naughty fun, but have we progressed in life only to find we are slipping back to some darker age in history when Nero played his fiddle while Rome burned? Where has sanity gone in our living? Is life truly all about greed, sex, and video games? Where has morality gone?

Where has political correctness taken us? Here's my answer. It has taken us to a political world of bureaucratic nonsense, keeping less than honest people in power because all they know is the subjugation of people. That's their game. If they can keep the people expecting all things from the government from cradle to grave, these less than honest people have won the game. They have their forever constituency and their power. Guess what? That's the secular mind-set…subjugation. They wish to create chaos with all that we believe and have come to cherish.

When they have won the game the secular progressives will have turned a hard-earned democracy into a social system of slavery – earn your money and give it to the state. Sound wacky? Maybe, all I have with which to work is this mind of mine and the minds of many others from whom I've seen what I believe to be the truth. Remember, Hitler and Nazi Germany was considered by many citizens too inane of purpose to last. Then, it became a paradigm for totalitarianism, a dictatorship.

What do we do about any of these things of which I speak? That is, can we stop secularism and socialism? I hope and pray we can.

It must start with a soft revolution of the American people. We must stop with the apathy and vigorously insist on changes in Washington, D. C. We must do a better job of vetting the people who work for us. There can be no mud-slinging in campaigns...the vetting should take care of the quality issues of candidates. Only policy issues can be debated. Once in the sacred halls of congress, those elected people who work for us, can have no contact with pressure groups, no lobbying by auto, cheese, milk, oil, or any other company on an issue that might be in the legislative mix. The people who work for us must sign an official affidavit of civility and honesty, with one strike and out. Each piece of legislation must be of one focus with no last minute add-on or 'pork' for a particular pet project of one state or another.

The states must take on a bigger role in stemming the size of our federal government, with the same affidavits of civility and honesty. There must be one question put on every piece of legislation in every seat of government, federal or state: 'Is this law good for the majority of our people?' The only answer can be yes. If it is not yes, the legislation is tabled or thrown out.

Whatever legislation is passed by the federal and state governments relative to private insurance coverage for individuals and/or groups must also apply to the representatives of the people. There can be no special perks for our government officials. Retirement packages must be similar to the private sector and transitional upon leaving after the term(s) served.

There should be term limits for our politicians. We have seen, depending on perspective, what longevity in public office has produced. A senator should serve one term of six years. A representative can serve a maximum of three terms, or, equal that to the term of a senator.

A federal budget must be set and met each year, just as the American families do. Trim the size of government and its many bureaucracies, combine some departments, but make or get under budget every year... I realize this sounds a bit ridiculous when we now stand at trillions of dollars over budget. If we stop the fraud in government, stop spending like those ever loving drunken sailors (ever loving because I was once a boy in blue!), stop the waste and pilfering of our treasury, a federal budget can be set and met.

Our tax system should be based on earnings and a consumption system with basic needs consumption not taxed. Earning taxes should be a flat tax with tiered ranges, the lowest of which has no tax. No Capital Gains taxes can be levied on the monies that have already been taxed. It is ludicrous when logic is applied: for example, my earnings have been taxed; from that net pay money I buy gas for the car (which is a taxable event), groceries for the family table (which is a taxable event); from that net pay money I put some money into an investment or a savings account, and I'm taxed again on the net money earnings. It is wrong and it should be changed.

Home ownership should not be burdened by excessive taxation. If a house has an assessed valuation system, say one-fourth of the market value, assuming taxes were paid on the house when purchased, assuming the homeowner is receiving some county services (fire, police, county officials, road, school, sewage, water, etc), taxes should never be more than one percent of the assessed value. There are variables to be considered. Some counties are small and have few revenue sources. Most counties provide fire and police protection but not always water, sewage, and road services. Adjustments for seniors in retirement should be made when their home is the only real estate owned and when they are on fixed incomes. Certain particular bills of exception should be part of the house taxation system.

No death taxes (estate taxes), period. I'm not rich and won't die rich so I face no such tax. But, again, the death tax is wrong and, no matter the wealth of an individual, her/his money should not be taxed at death. It is an ugly and vile tax, particularly when one considers all the multiple taxation of our money, not to mention the fraud and waste matters of government.

As we have now, we should remain the mightiest military power on the face of the earth. There is no better security for our country than by having a strong military force, with the most state of the art equipment and the most intelligent people running our armed forces. Our CIA, NSA, FBI all of our intelligence gathering agencies should be second to no other nation in the world.

We do these things and more and we can hopefully put the progressive activists and the anything-goes crowd on the move – preferably to other socialist countries that will listen to their half-truths and no truths. That is after all their goal, to throw our beloved nation into chaos, to push us toward a destiny other countries and cultures have met – destruction of the human spirit and domination of the power-hungry elite.

Whether you agree or not, I believe our current president is among that liberal elite crowd. He deceives us with his untruths and with his constant complaining about the bad guys on the right. He is a constant campaigner with no desire to lead this nation in a thoughtful and meaningful way. He is a charming piece of arrogance who fools so many along the way. He cannot, will not, tell us about Benghazi, about Fast and Furious, about the IRS targeting of conservative groups like The Tea Party, and now he is slapping us in the face with his

Obamacare, and, out of his own ignorance of the bill or just knowing in his haughty strides that he's in his second term and can't be touched, refusing to own up to his falsehoods that 'you can keep your old insurance plan if you want', that 'it's grandfathered in', that 'you can keep your doctor'. President Obama recently danced around an apology for his remarks, but it was all self-serving mush. The man cannot accept blame for his actions. Rather he will somehow blame the insurance companies that have worked for years to bring health policies up to his Obamacare mandates. Of course, there will also be blame stones cast at his right wing adversaries.

Could I be wrong about the so-called Affordable Care Act'? Am I and others wrong that this act will do for the president and the secular progressives what was intended all along --- bankrupt our nation and push us further toward his socialistic dream? Perhaps this time next year, Obamacare will be running smoothly, saving people lots of money, and lots of doctors singing its praises.

JOE PUBLIC'S POLITICAL PERSPECTIVE

Perhaps this time next year, rabbits will fly.

11) Where Do You Want To Go From Here?

Okay, guess I've been a little rough around the edges, but needed to get some stuff off my chest, maybe contribute in the political debate of our country instead of sitting in the wings. Though I did some acting back in the day, no star-quality stuff, I likely would not be writing any of this if I was a Hollywood star or show business personality. The showbiz peeps are there to entertain us, not to use their celebrity to further a biased cause or a preferred candidate – though it is certainly their right to do so. There have been a few of my favorite actors I do not watch anymore because they've become political activists. I am not an activist, just a private citizen who wanted to let the world know how I feel about something as important as the direction and drift of my country. I also want my kids, grandkids, and their kids to know how I feel about my country and the pride I have in the United States of America.

So, other than away from me, where do you want to go from here? Do you want to go to a place where there is some sanity, some common sense, in the way business is handled in our government?

If you need something particular, like new furniture for your home, you will no doubt shop around various store outlets until you find what it is you are looking. For a particular car model you will shop the dealers who inventory the brand... This could be a bad example because car sales people get picked on a lot... Then, again, this could be a perfect example since we are talking politics. The point is, in all of our life dealings, we want to deal with someone who will give us fair and honest value for our money.

In Politics the concept should not be so different. We elect, hire, our public servants to give us fair and honest value for our money that they will end up spending. The process for electing, hiring, public servants is without question different from hiring a contractor, a plumber, a landscaper. We usually check with our neighbor and get a reference or we look in a book of yellow pages. In politics there is a totally different and lengthy process, unless someone is appointed or otherwise through some protocol is appointed.

A man, a woman, filled with ambition, great ideas, and ideals files papers to run for an office, say congressman/congresswoman, and the name goes on the ballot. There begins a period of serious campaigning, where the man/woman tells the constituents what he/she feels are the important issues facing the district, the state, the country. There may be public debates. There will be advertising of all kinds – print, radio, TV. The day of the election arrives. Votes are cast. The man or woman is elected and feels the thrill of victory.

The elected man/woman goes to Washington, is overwhelmed with the history as he/she strolls the hallowed halls. The elected person feels the electrifying and subtle tingles of power as they meet elder statesmen/stateswomen and the anticipation of greatness to come is mixed with some humility and tension.

It is not long before the newbie congress person is introduced to the *quid pro quo* world of politics, where sometimes honesty and integrity clash with comity and opportunity. So much new filtered and unfiltered data can almost devastate the newbie, so much not heretofore known about the kept secrets of the *Beltway*. There is so much to be done, so much taxpayer money to be spent for this program or project. Here the newbie learns the nuances and hard truths of conciliation, of contending left/right opinions.

So it is then a house and a senate of constant contention, of hand shakes and approvals, of winning and losing. What I believe happens is that so much of what occurs in Washington becomes personal, to the point that we the people are perhaps forgotten in the battles that ensue. There is one very important acknowledgement to make. It is our system of government. It is our democracy in action, and, for the most part, it works very well. But, on occasion, we eat too much pork and at times the baby is thrown out with the bath water.

Please note that this book is weighed heavily against the current president and some of his faithful. In no way do I aim to imply that the republicans are all good guys... They are fighting among themselves, the moderates and The Tea Party. They, too, are spending our hard-earned money. In many ways they are adding to the frustration and angst. It is just that I subscribe to the principles of the Republican Party – less government in my face, less taxation and a simple tax code, strong military, family values, et al.

So, where do you want to go from here? How do you want to improve this time-sacred form of government? How does it get so far out of whack as it appears to be right now? Since I'm doing the writing here, let me put some words down and see if you agree or disagree with a Joe Public scenario of change.

First of all, a business in this or any country needs a leader. Our three branches of government is a business. Ergo, we need a leader. It is my Joe Public opinion that we do not have a leader at this time in our history. We have a president of great charm and a gift of eloquent speaking, and I believe he does have a vision for our country, misguided though it might be. But he is not a leader.

A leader can delegate authority to position heads, but he must still know the fundamental character of each position and what transpires there. He must be able to account for the actions of his people in any department. (Cases in point: Attorney General Eric Holder in the DOJ and 'Fast and Furious; Kathleen Sibeleus in the HHS and her ineptitude; the president himself and his promises of citizens being able to keep their doctor and their insurance.) In my opinion, therein lies a primary fault of this president.

For the most part, President Obama has named people to important power posts who are either inept and/or without a moral compass. In previous sections I've mentioned some of these areas. The president has many news conferences where he takes five or ten minutes to answer or maneuver a question he has been asked to a point of incongruity. He seemingly cannot answer a question without equivocating.

There is a reason for that. He can talk and roll his words into several topics which are most favorable to him and the original question did not identify.

It is important that a president of the United States, a leader, be able to work amiably with both sides of the political aisle. Obama does not, has not, done this. How can a bill like the Affordable Care Act pass and not have one Republican vote? How many times have we heard that the president wants to meet with the Republicans in the house or senate? There have been times, but, those moments were spent mostly with the president usually dictating his stances, not really seeking advice and/or legislative ideas. So, this president has not sought counsel from all of the People's elected representatives, generally just those from his party.

The world is most definitely watching the United States and its president's actions. From what I read and see, our esteem and respect has gone down considerably in the world. A leader, particularly of this nation, must keep us militarily strong and keep our allies firmly and faithfully in camp. Our leader must not vacillate on matters of international importance. We have seen this president waver on issues in Libya and Syria, have not heard him brief us on the fatal Benghazi attack and killings after a full year has passed. The president, like his rambling news conferences, parses his words into phraseology we have now come to expect: 'We will find those responsible and hold them responsible…' But we never get that e-mail!

So, in my opinion, we need a leader, a person with both charisma and with the critical leadership tools to run a nation, someone who intelligently plans his work and works his plan.

On both sides can we stop with the 'pork'? Can we <u>not</u> add on to a bill some 'bridge to nowhere'? Can we get serious about the spending of the people's tax dollars? Can we not have a firm 'check list' of DO NOTS on what to include in a piece of legislation – with each representative signing an affidavit? Can we not take a look at the way we structure laws, making sure the American people are in every thought process? Can we not stop access to politicians by lobbyists and people of selfish persuasion? Can we not have a new type of Newt Gingrich 'promise list' that will offer a course of action to our citizens?

Can our government representatives not live by the laws we the people live? (Same insurance plans, same retirement stipulations, etc.)

Can we not possibly pass legislation that will make the promises made by the President regarding ACA come to pass? ('If you like your doctor and your insurance plan, you can keep it!') Can the insurance companies, without more costly government subsidies, afford to comply with such legislation and with random ACA executive order decisions? Can we not just repeal this arcane and massive ACA legislation? We lose dollars. We lose doctors. We lose our freedom of choice. How can a huge bureaucracy know better than we the people what is good for us? Do not force us to eat from the government trough.

How about you? Where do you want to go from here? No matter your side, you surely want freedom and liberty. You surely don't want to give up your right to choices you might want to make.

Maybe Democrats and Republicans need to define themselves better. I can't believe our good citizens want to go the route of Socialism, where an elite few in power rake in the money and see to our needs cradle to grave. Sweden does very well in its Socialized country, but they are small. The United States is too large for such a system – Socialism can only lead us to anarchy and totalitarianism. At least, that is the way I see it.

I am but one voice. You have yours. Ultimately, in our future, it will be the voices heard loudest that will run the victory laps.

12) Some Last Thoughts

It has always been difficult to wrap my simple mind around the 'conspiracy theories' that some people come to believe. Of course they are interesting to ponder, and, looking back through history there have been many taken out of theory and placed into fact.

The JFK assassination has produced many 'conspiracy theories' but the majority of people still believe that Lee Harvey Oswald was the lone killer of the much loved president whose name has become synonymous with Camelot. I was young then and President Kennedy was indeed charismatic and brought a certain needed spirit back to the people. JFK held me spellbound along with so many millions of others. With the passage of fifty years, the conspiracy theories are still out there – CIA, Mafia, Castro, Johnson – along with many adherents.

Here I've included some articles related to President Obama that may well be intellectually honest and sincerely believed by many people. Wayne Allyn Root's article taken from the Las Vegas Review-Journal, April, 2013, is one that is most compelling to me. Yet, my mind cannot totally accept the fact that a man with such charisma and eloquence as President Obama could be manipulating the United States and its people in an effort to corrupt our economy, our ideals, our Constitution, in leading us to a state of subjugation that renders our freedom and liberty relatively non-existent.

Does it make sense? Yes, it makes much too much sense. Scary sense! When one watches the current events play out, the relative arrogance of the Democratic Party, the nuclear option of a Democratically-controlled Senate that breaks 225 years of a manifest agreement, the 100 % partisan legacy legislation we euphemistically call ObamaCare, the refusal to compromise of a most superior-sounding president and his failure to acknowledge his increasing disfavor among the American people because of his lack of leadership and his inept group of party advisors, when these events and behavior patterns present themselves there is most assuredly problems in our good country. There is most assuredly a move toward a single-party nanny mentality that could cripple, even destroy our way of life.

Perhaps the Republicans are not pure of heart and mind, but I do feel they are more compassionate to the needs of the people. All people! It has been a favorite sport of Democrats and like-minded people to paint the portrait of Republicans as the rich and uncaring party. The minorities listen to the falsehoods of the Democrats because it appears they will get a better break. What the minorities do not realize is that their freedom and liberty are being chipped away by the deception and liberal mindset of a group of politicians that are interested only in their power bases.

The president and many in the political ranks have never run a business, never had to set a budget and stand by it. The only working life many of these people have known is politics.

Yes, it is true in both parties but far more faithful to fact in the Democratic camp.

My words come from a conservative place. My mindset is Republican because it is a conservative party. It is a party that believes less government is the best government. It is a party that believes heartily in the free enterprise system, in Capitalism, in the rights of people to work and achieve as far as their talents take them. It is a party that believes too much taxation stifles the growth of our economy. It is a party that believes the states and local areas should handle many of the issues that face them, not the federal government. It is a party that is passionate and caring, a party that realizes there are people, old, handicapped, infirm, who need the government's help. To listen to a Democrat, a Republican has no heart. Republicans do have a heart! And, Republicans have a mind knowing that too much welfare, too much bureaucratic wasteful spending, and too many pay-outs of government checks due to fraud, can cripple our economy.

I've had my days in the sun. I've taken advantage of government welfare. I've never been a workaholic, but I've worked enough to achieve modest successes. I can understand how one could honestly and dishonestly be lured to food stamps and the welfare system. As I mentioned earlier, welfare might, by needs directed, be a nice place to visit but I surely do not wish to stay there too long.

If there is any ultimate message to my ramblings here, it is this: *Do not be seduced by the politicians who promise you a free ride through life – there is no way that promise can be kept.* It might be hackneyed but it is still true, if you give an honest effort with the talent God gives and you can possibly avoid the government dole, your life will have more meaning.

A few more things and my writing here will end.

This 'Joe Public' exercise is a bit like 'anger management' as I try to grasp all the bits and pieces that make up our current federal government. My words were never intended to become a tome where every conceivable issue in Washington was covered. As mentioned in my opening, I'm part of this wonderful country and I'm exercising my God-given right to express my views. The views might not be presented in a civil and orderly manner as perhaps a political pundit or analyst might present, but they are mine and I make no apologies for what I've written.

I've been hard on President Barack Obama and his party. Mr. Obama's vision for America does not fit my vision but he does live in the land of the free and has the right to believe as he will. As a President of this country he works for all of us and he should listen to the majority of Americans and get away from his constant campaigning about how government knows better than the people what is best. He should try being less political in all he does and try leading us away from bankrupting this nation. With our country trillions of dollars in debt and his legacy law, the Affordable Healthcare Act, becoming more and more expensive as I tap my laptop keys – one-sixth of our economy – I'm voicing concerns held by the majority. The US Constitution was written to protect the minorities against the whims of the majority, and, this I get. But when that protection of the minorities becomes more than it was meant to be, the concerns I've put forth here have some major meaning, I truly believe.

I am seeing my beloved country almost unrecognizable to me. A President of color has been elected twice by the people and still we have those who raise issues of race and bias. We will always have some loony tune folks railing on the matter of race, but, for me, I'm tired of some government representatives, so-called minority leaders, and a press that keeps stirring the cauldron of hate and divisiveness.

There are some ugly events taking place in the US, and a government bent on entitlements and redistribution of wealth is only adding to the menu of problems. The media hardly covers certain issues because political correctness has run amok. We have some young groups of people playing a deadly game of 'knockout' where men and women, old and young, walking along minding their business are knocked out by a brutal blow. The young group walks on, and the national leaders of political clout and those in the media of the liberal persuasion hardly feel it is newsworthy... So much I've already mentioned, but it is a country I find difficult to understand. There is an incipient fear within me of this nation's ultimate direction.

So I rant, rave, and feel like maybe I've gotten it all off my chest. Silly me! It will still be there tomorrow with another sound bite of news, one side saying this, the other polar opposite. What is to become of us, our country? Are we in the end by government's action come to civil unrest, perhaps choose our sides and fight again as we once did in the great civil war? Can we learn nothing from history? Can our esteemed college/university theorists dream up new ways of causing radical social change and channel it through future political leaders? Has history taught us nothing about the types of government that only debase its people and bring eventual chaos and ruin?

We have a democracy and a wonderful blueprint for keeping our political train on track. It's called the US Constitution. We've had problems in the past that divided our union, and it took a bloody war to correct one of them. Perhaps I'm too simple a man but I believe we can keep our democracy alive and well with good and honest people running the government locomotive who truly do have our best interests at heart.

In any event, this is my long letter to every House Representative and every Senator who would lend an ear to an old Joe Public...

Each of you <u>and</u> the President serve us and at our pleasure.

Stop giving yourselves benefits not available to our citizenry.

Stop catering to special interest groups that only benefit a few.

Make new Union Laws that can stop the money and power hungry leaders...perhaps we can compete better with global markets.

Provide for meaningful educational options for spending our dollars, whether they are in the form of voucher system, charter schools with a vocational base, special learning centers, et al. Stop feeding our money into an NEA that does not give us the best bang for our bucks.

Start reading the laws you put together and thoroughly understand them.

Begin believing once again that power does indeed corrupt and keep uppermost in your minds the American people in every action you take.

Please stop the entitlement frenzy. We now have laws that provide for the needy among us and we no doubt have to do more. Allow the local and state governments to determine those in their areas who legitimately need assistance. Most of us want no centralized monolith to make these decisions. Certainly, with our technology, we can determine those who would corrupt a common sense system of rules and regulations, those who would scheme with criminal intent to rob our treasuries.

Simplify our tax laws with a flat tax that is fairly tiered.

Keep our borders and our people safe and secure with a strong military and a non-partisan, workable immigration law.

Please get rid of the Affordable Care Act – it is a disaster waiting to happen and not for this great country.

By all means, keep God and Government separate but do not mock the faith majority with politically correct denials of their rituals and their holidays.

My dear daughter sent me an e-mail the other day which had more observations by the man I quoted earlier in this book – Wayne Allyn Root. This I leave for you to ponder whether or not there is truth to these observations, or, simply 'sour grapes'. Mr. Root is an astute political commentator and a conservative with a distinctive resume. It appears he will likely run as a Republican for a US Senate seat in Nevada in the 2016 election. I include his comments for your consideration.

177

There are also some closing remarks from a feisty 21-year old lady from Texas. Her comments have appeared in previous E-mails, but just in case you missed them, they follow Mr. Root. To my mind, there is wisdom in what she has to say.

With these final observations, you may close my book, walk away angry with my comments or walk away with some hopeful sense of compatible reassurance. In either scenario, be assured these are my heartfelt and honest reflections.

*

There are two major political parties in America. I'm a member of the naïve, stupid, and cowardly one. I'm a Republican.

Why ObamaCare is a fantastic success

By Wayne Allyn Root

Published October 21, 2013

FoxNews.com

How stupid is the GOP? They still don't get it. I told them 5 years ago, 2 books ago, a national bestseller ago ("The Ultimate Obama Survival Guide"), and in hundreds of articles and commentaries, that ObamaCare was never meant to help America, or heal the sick, or lower healthcare costs, or lower the debt, or expand the economy.

The GOP needs to stop calling ObamaCare a "trainwreck." That means it's a mistake, or accident. That means it's a gigantic flop, or failure. It's NOT.

Message to the GOP: This isn't a game. This isn't tiddly-winks. This is a serious, purposeful attempt to highjack America and destroy capitalism.

This is a brilliant, cynical, and purposeful attempt to damage the U.S. economy, kill jobs, and bring down capitalism.

It's not a failure, it's Obama's grand success.

It's not a "trainwreck," ObamaCare is a suicide attack. He wants to hurt us, to bring us to our knees, to capitulate - so we agree under duress to accept big government.

Obama's hero and mentor was Saul Alinsky -- a radical Marxist intent on destroying capitalism. Alinksky's stated advice was to call the other guy "a terrorist" to hide your own intentions.

To scream that the other guy is "ruining America," while you are the one actually plotting the destruction of America. To claim again and again...in every sentence of every speech...that you are "saving the middle class," while you are busy wiping out the middle class.

The GOP is so stupid they can't see it. There are no mistakes here. This is a planned purposeful attack.

The tell-tale sign isn't the disastrous start to ObamaCare. Or the devastating effect the new taxes are having on the economy. Or the death of full-time jobs. Or the overwhelming debt. Or the dramatic increases in health insurance rates. Or the 70% of doctors now thinking of retiring- bringing on a healthcare crisis of unimaginable proportions. Forget all that.

The real sign that this is a purposeful attack upon capitalism is how many Obama administration members and Democratic Congressmen are openly calling Tea Party Republicans and anyone who wants to stop ObamaCare "terrorists."

There's the clue. Even the clueless GOP should be able to see that.

They are calling the reasonable people...the patriots...the people who believe in the Constitution ... the people who believe exactly what the Founding Fathers believed...the people who want to take power away from corrupt politicians who have put America $17 trillion in debt...terrorists?

That's because they are Saul Alinsky-ing the GOP. The people trying to purposely hurt America, capitalism and the middle class...are calling the patriots by a terrible name to fool, confuse and distract the public.

ObamaCare is a raving, rollicking, fantastic success. Stop calling it a failure. Here is what it was created to do. It is succeeding on all counts:

1. ObamaCare was intended to bring about the Marxist dream -- redistribution of wealth. *Rich people, small business owners, and the middle class are being robbed, so that the money can be redistributed to poor people (who vote for Democrats).*

Think about it. If you're rich or middle class, you now have to pay for your own health care costs (at much higher rates) <u>AND</u> 40 million other people's costs too (through massive tax increases).

So you're stuck paying for both bills. You are left broke. Brilliant.

2. ObamaCare was intended to wipe out the middle class and make them dependent on government.
Think about it. Even Obama's IRS predicts that health insurance for a typical American family by 2016 will be $20,000 per year. But how would middle class Americans pay that bill and have anything left for food or housing or living?

People that make $40K, or $50K, or $60K can't possibly hope to spend $20K on health insurance without becoming homeless.

Bingo. That's how you make middle class people dependent on government. That's how you make everyone addicted to government checks. Brilliant.

3. As a bonus, ObamaCare is intended to kill every decent paying job in the economy, creating only crummy, crappy part-time jobs. *Why? Just to make sure the middle class is trapped, with no way out. Just to make sure no one has the $20,000 per year to pay for health insurance, thereby guaranteeing they become wards of the state. Brilliant.*

4. ObamaCare is intended to bankrupt small business, and therefore starve donations to the GOP.
Think about it. Do you know a small business owner? I know hundreds of them. Their rates are being doubled, tripled and quadrupled by ObamaCare.

Guess who writes 75% of the checks to Republican candidates and conservative causes? Small Business.

Even if a small business owner manages to survive, he or she certainly can't write a big check to the GOP anymore. Money is the "mother's milk" of politics. Without donations, a political party ceases to exist. Bingo.

That's the point of ObamaCare. Obama is bankrupting his political opposition and drying up donations to the GOP. Brilliant.

5. ObamaCare is intended to make the IRS all-powerful.
It adds thousands of new IRS agents. It puts the IRS in charge of overseeing 15% of the U.S. economy. The IRS has the right because of ObamaCare to snoop into every aspect of your life, to go into your bank accounts, to fine you, to frighten you, to intimidate you. And Obama and his socialist cabal have access to your deepest medical secrets.

By law your doctor has to ask your sexual history. That information is now in the hands of

Obama and the IRS to blackmail GOP candidates into either not running, or supporting bigger government, or leaking the info and ruining your campaign.

Or have you forgotten the IRS harassed, intimidated and persecuted critics of Obama and conservative groups?

Now Obama hands the IRS even more power. Big Brother rules our lives. Brilliant.

6. ObamaCare is intended to unionize 15 million healthcare workers.
That produces $15 billion in new union dues. That money goes to fund Democratic candidates and socialist causes -- thereby guaranteeing Obama's friends never lose another election, and Obama's policies keep ruining capitalism and bankrupting business owners long after he's out of office.

Message to the GOP: This isn't a game. This isn't tiddly-winks. This is a serious, purposeful attempt to highjack America and destroy capitalism.

185

JOE PUBLIC'S POLITICAL PERSPECTIVE

This isn't a trainwreck. It's purposeful suicide.

It's not failing, it's working exactly according to plan. Obama knows what he's doing. Stop apologizing and start fighting.

Oh and one more thing...Conservatives aren't "terrorists." We are patriots and saviors. We represent the Constitution and the Founding Fathers. We are the heroes and good guys. Unless you get all this through your thick skulls, America is lost...forever.

*

Finally, a young Texas lady expresses her feelings:

This was written by a 21 year old female who gets it. It's her future she's worried about and this is how she feels about the social welfare big government state that she's being forced to live in! These solutions are just common sense in her opinion.

This was in the Waco Tribune Herald, Waco , TX Nov 18

JOE PUBLIC'S POLITICAL PERSPECTIVE

Put me in charge ...

Put me in charge of food stamps. I'd get rid of Lone Star cards; no cash for Ding Dongs or Ho Ho's, just money for 50-pound bags of rice and beans, blocks of cheese and all the powdered milk you can haul away. If you want steak and frozen pizza, then get a job.

Put me in charge of Medicaid. The first thing I'd do is to get women Norplant birth control implants or tubal ligation. Then, we'll test recipients for drugs, alcohol, and nicotine. If you want to reproduce or use drugs, alcohol, or smoke, then get a job.

Put me in charge of government housing. Ever live in a military barracks?

You will maintain our property in a clean and good state of repair. Your "home" will be subject to inspections anytime and possessions will be inventoried. If you want a plasma TV or Xbox 360, then get a job and your own place.

JOE PUBLIC'S POLITICAL PERSPECTIVE

In addition, you will either present a check stub from a job each week or you will report to a "government" job. It may be cleaning the roadways of trash, painting and repairing public housing, whatever we find for you We will sell your 22 inch rims and low profile tires and your blasting stereo and speakers and put that money toward the "common good.."

Before you write that I've violated someone's rights, realize that all of the above is voluntary. If you want our money, accept our rules.. Before you say that this would be "demeaning" and ruin their "self esteem," consider that it wasn't that long ago that taking someone Else's money for doing absolutely nothing was demeaning and lowered self esteem.

If we are expected to pay for other people's mistakes we should at least attempt to make them learn from their bad choices. The current system rewards them for continuing to make bad choices.

AND, while you are on government Assistance, you no longer can VOTE! Yes that is correct.

For you to vote would be a conflict of interest. You will voluntarily remove yourself from voting while you are receiving a government welfare check. If you want to vote, then get a job.

*

Ranting and raving can get a lot off the chest <u>and</u> hurt some feelings. I have some good friends who believe just as fervently in their liberal views as I do in my conservative views… I hope they are still my friends.

That is what much of our lives are about – sharing our views with each other, given that it is difficult to remain completely within our halo of congeniality when discussing religion and politics.

While he could very likely care less, Charles Krauthammer is my Conservative hero. Dr. Krauthammer has recently published a book entitled, *Things That Matter,* currently <u>number one</u> on the New York Time's Best Seller List. There are so many delightful quotes that I could use from this book of personal and political potpourri to put a lovely final touch on this rather pedestrian essay of mine, but I shall not invade his space. Suffice, if you really and truly want to read about Conservative philosophy, you must read the books of this remarkable, witty, and most wise man.

The 'simple man', Bill O'Reilly, does not always please 'the folks' with his 'no spin' comments on the news of the day, but he is a good man and I believe he honestly and with his own flair does 'look out' for us, makes sure we the people know 360 degrees of an issue. He gives so much to charities which he checks out thoroughly. His books are instant best sellers and have much historical value. He does not suffer charlatans and fools easily and he is there each day 'looking out' for his fellow citizens. In my humble opinion, you can take to the bank what he tells you.

There are other political heroes for me on both sides of the aisle, living and dead… John F. Kennedy meant so much to me in my younger days, truly the man from Camelot who gave me a sense of pride and hope. Like everyman he made good and bad decisions, but he was a true patriot. When he was taken from us in an awful way, I mourned with the rest of the country…no nation has mourned so much.

There are so many who have chosen to live in the arena of ideas, to give us their viewpoints on the major issues of the day, to espouse their causes. In most cases, if not all, they believe what they tell us, what they write for us. We choose our favorites because their words strike a chord in our hearts and minds, or, maybe, their persuasion reaches us through our DNA, through our heritage.

Who is right? Who is wrong? We have two major political parties. Are the Republicans right? Are the Democrats right? Are the far left secular progressives right? Are the far right Neo-Nazi thinkers of appeal to some?

For me, coming as no surprise, I'm a fully in-tune Conservative, believing superfluously that we cannot be all things to all people. A big government, big world, conglomerate that controls our lives has no appeal for me. Small is better than big so far as governments are concerned. Give me freedom and liberty to make choices and build my life the best I can. The people who work for all of us, the people we elect to run the affairs we cannot, those who are empowered to protect our shores and provide the basic laws and programs to keep us human, those people must be of pure heart and neutral mind with no planned mandates that fit another political system. We have our political system, wrought by founding fathers whom were wise and far-reaching in their wisdom, wrought through hardships and through abandonment of their prior homelands where they faced persecution and little privilege.

Some of us hurt through no fault of our own. We need to count on our government for help. Some of us just make it. Some of us make it big through hard work and sacrifice. We are all on this same sacred land we call the United States. To the extent we can, we must help our ailing neighbor – hopefully through the private communities where we live. It just seems wrong when we mandate by complex laws like the AHA that we give up our entrepreneurial spirit, our incentive to be all we can be, for the idea of equality for the masses. We have laws that help those in need. We can do more, but not through a cumbersome law that can bankrupt our nation.

But that is the intrigue of politics. It seems at times our lives veritably stem from that awkward science. History can certainly prove that point. Take a close look at nearby Cuba, at Hitler's Germany, at modern Greece, at much of Europe and the Middle East, farther back at the Roman civilization. Do you believe that is where we should be going?

Right or wrong, I have given you my 'Joe Public' views. My little book is not broad in scope but, for the most part, it scratches the surfaces I wished to scratch.

Civility is now again on the table…

THE END